Prophe(

Prophetic Words & Divine Revelations

For You, the Church and the Nations

An End-Time Prophet's Journal

* * * = MUST READ

Michael Backholer

Prophecy Now, Prophetic Words and Divine Revelations
for You, the Church and the Nations
An End-Time Prophet's Journal

- Jesus Christ is Lord -

Contents

Page   **Chapter**

After the Spirit had rested on the elders of Israel, and they prophesied, Moses replying to Joshua, said, "Are you zealous for my sake? Oh, that all the Lord's people were prophets and that the Lord would put His Spirit on them" (Numbers 11:29).

Moses said to the children of Israel, "The Lord your God will raise up for you a Prophet like me from your midst, from your brethren. Him you shall hear" (Deuteronomy 18:15). This was JESUS CHRIST via the seed of King David.

Thus says the Lord, "And it shall come to pass afterward that I will pour out My Spirit on all flesh; your sons and your daughters shall prophesy, your old men shall dream dreams, your young men shall see visions; and also on My menservants and My maidservants I will pour out My Spirit in those days" (Joel 2:28-29).

Foreword

'For we know in part and we prophesy in part' (1 Cor. 13:9).

This book is no ordinary book as words from the Holy Spirit have been communicated to man. This book is chronologically based, but chapters have been inserted to give structure, whilst related revelations and prophecies are together. This has not always been easy, as many of the 'words' cover multiple issues or subjects, but where clear patterns and themes have emerged, this has been done. Many of the 'words' have had a subtitle added as a quick reference to explain the main theme or essence of what each prophecy or revelation is about.

Some chapters contain 'boxed' text, which is interspersed throughout a number of chapters. These additions were not given with the prophecy or revelation, but are either verses from the Holy Bible, or text, which have been inserted to complement or help explain some spiritual truths.

This book contains many spiritual truths, but no new doctrine, as doctrine is found in the Word of God, the Holy Bible, and *not* in prophecy. Each prophecy / revelation is firmly grounded in the Word of God and the author is accountable to other Christian leaders who have weighed and judged each word within this book. Read the Holy Bible, apply it and live it – go and proclaim the glad tidings of Jesus Christ and point them firmly to Calvary, to the bloodstained cross; repentance and faith in Jesus Christ.

The name Michael Backholer, date of the prophecy or revelation and website www.ProphecyNow.co.uk are given under each word. People may wish to photocopy some of the prophecies or revelations to pass around, print in a newsletter, pray into, hand to a friend, give to a church leader, or to post on their websites, blogs or social media web pages – an original source is *always* needed for accountability and authenticity. No prophecy is of private interpretation, & distribution is permitted and encouraged for non-financial gain *with* full accreditation. These words can also be viewed at www.ProphecyNow.co.uk.

The Publisher

Preface

On the Day of Pentecost, Peter, stood up with the eleven, raised his voice and said to those gathered, "...These are not drunk as you suppose, since it is only the third hour of the day. But this is what was spoken by the Prophet Joel, 'And it shall come to pass in the last days, says God that I will pour out of My Spirit on all flesh; your sons and daughters shall prophesy, your young men shall see visions, your old men shall dream dreams. And on My menservants and on My maidservants I will pour out My Spirit in those days' " (Acts 2:14-18).

It never entered my mind to write a book and in many respects, I have not. I spoke and wrote as the Spirit gave utterance, and have tried to be faithful to all that the Holy Spirit has revealed to me in and through each prophecy and revelation (2 Peter 1:21). These words can be found on my website www.ProphecyNow.co.uk, alongside any future ones.

Sometimes these revelations or prophecies are given in quick succession, at other times, months can pass before I receive a word from the Holy Spirit that has to be put down in writing. Some are plain and easy to understand, others are not. Some have a play on words, or rhyme has been incorporated, whilst others can have two meanings or are written as a riddle, and are designed to be thought over and pondered (Mark 4:11-13 and 1 Corinthians 2:14). Yet others are given in figurative language (John 16:25), whilst some are analogies or allegories – living parables.

All are edifying, to build up, however some are pointed and are an indictment to the Body of Christ – the Church, and many professing Christians, and even Christian workers. 'Do not despise the chastening of the Lord...nor be discouraged when you are rebuked by Him, for whom the Lord loves, He chastens...' (Hebrews 12:5-6).

Many of the prophecies, the visions and revelations of revival (especially in the first two chapters), can be prayed over to see the fulfilment of the will of the Lord, to 'pour our His Spirit' (Joel 2:28) and to 'pour water on him who is thirsty and floods upon the dry ground' (Isaiah 44:3). In the same way that Daniel understood that Jerusalem, and its surrounding land, would be desolate for seventy years according to the Word of the Lord under Jeremiah the prophet (Jeremiah 25:11-12). Knowing that the time had been fulfilled, Daniel prayed for Jerusalem to be repaired and re-inhabited (Daniel 4:2-4). He 'stood in the gap' (Ezekiel 22:30) on behalf of the people, prayed, fasted and made confession to God for his sins, the sins of his forefathers, and pleaded for God to fulfil His Word (Daniel 4:3-19).

Many of the revelations and prophecies contain direct lines of Scripture, or paraphrases of verses from the Holy Bible, which many will relate and recall; they will ring true, even if you are not familiar with the particular passage of Scripture. For others, verses from the Holy Bible may be seen in a different light, perhaps even a violation of their *own* theology, but it is the Holy Spirit who guides into all truth and glorifies Jesus Christ (John 16:13). Jesus said, "My doctrine is not Mine, but His who sent Me" (John 7:16), and Jesus was constantly about His Father's business, and is one with Him. Jesus contended with the Sadducees (who denied the resurrection) and plainly told them, "You are mistaken, not knowing the Scriptures nor the power of God" (Matthew 22:29). Peter received a vision from God, relating to Cornelius, a Roman centurion who feared God. The vision, and then meeting illuminated what the Scriptures said about the Gentiles; they were not common or unclean, and would become part of the family of God, a reiteration of the words of the prophets, and the Holy Spirit fell! (Acts 10-11:18 and Romans 1:2-3). As God spoke to Abraham, 'In you, all nations of the earth will be blessed' (Genesis 12:3b).

In order to test prophecy be like the Bereans who 'searched the Scriptures daily,' to see if what had been said was true (Acts 17:11), and let us be 'doers of the Word, and not hearers only,' otherwise we deceive ourselves (James 1:22).

'You also, as living stones, are being built up a spiritual house, a holy priesthood, to offer up spiritual sacrifices acceptable to God through Jesus Christ.... You are a chosen generation, a royal priesthood, a holy nation, His own special people, that you may proclaim the praises of Him who called you out of darkness into His marvellous light' (1 Peter 2:5, 9).

Michael Backholer, June 2013

The Author (From the Publisher)

'Do not quench the Spirit. Do not despise prophecies' (1 Thessalonians 5:19-20).

Michael was born in the South of England, a few years after the end of World War II. As a teenager, he fell in love with God and always knew that the Lord had a call upon his life though was not born again, nor God-fearing till his mid thirties. In the early eighties, Michael fully surrendered his life to Jesus Christ and came into the fullness of the Holy Spirit.

In 1989, he was called into the hidden life and was released from working for an earthly master. Since that time, whilst based in the UK, he has also served the Lord in the USA, South Africa, Poland, France, Ireland and all over Great Britain. Michael has often been sought by church leaders and Christian workers for advice, prophetic insight, prayer and ministry.

In June 1989, whilst on a mission in Scotland, Michael received a vision of revival. At North Queensferry, very early one morning, having been wakened by the Lord. He walked down near the water and was looking up at the majestic Forth Bridge, when the Lord said, "I had these bridges [one is for trains and the other for vehicles] built for the same reason the Roman roads were built – for the spread of My gospel." Suddenly as Michael looked up, he saw flames of fire appearing hundreds of feet high, flowing across the bridge from north to south. In astonishment he said, "What is it Lord?" having never received a vision before. "It's flames of revival, I'm going to send revival and it will start in the north and flow south," replied the Lord.

Michael never lost sight of the promise of revival, which has been relayed on many Christian channels, and continues to believe that the greatest Christian revival is yet to come. "God is not a man, that He should lie, nor a son of man that He should repent. Has He not said, and will He not do it? Or has He spoken, and will He not make it good?" (Num. 23:19), NKJV.

The author receives no financial recompense for this book, but has requested that all royalties be invested into the Kingdom of God, for evangelism, missions, discipleship and Bibles etc.

UNDERSTAND WHAT you
READ & **An Introduction to Prophecy** WHY

'We also have the prophetic word made sure, which you do well to heed as a light that shines in a dark place, until the day dawns and the morning star rises in your hearts, knowing this first, that no prophecy of Scripture is of private interpretation, for prophecy never came by the will of man, but holy men of God spoke as they were moved by the Holy Spirit' (2 Peter 1:19-21).

Understanding Prophecy and Prophetic Words
1. Prophecy is an important gift for the Body of Christ and must not be despised, disregarded or neglected, but heeded.
- 'Pursue love, and desire spiritual gifts, but especially that you may prophesy' (1 Corinthians 14:1).
- 'He who prophesies speaks edification and exhortation and comfort to men...he who prophesies edifies the Church' (1 Corinthians 14:3-4). To edify means to 'build up,' and a word of rebuke (spoken in love) is edifying as godly sorrow can lead to repentance (2 Corinthians 7:10). C.f. Proverbs 6:23b and Proverbs 27:5.
- 'Do not quench the Spirit. Do not despise prophecies' (1 Thessalonians 5:19-20).

2. Prophecy needs to be weighed, judged, often prayed through and tested, because many false prophets, and deceiving, lying spirits are in the world, trying to deceive and beguile.
- 'Test all things; hold fast what is good' (1 Thessalonians 5:21).
- 'Beloved, do not believe every spirit, but test the spirits, whether they are of God; because many false prophets have gone out into the world' (1 John 4:1).

3. A prophecy can be from God, of the flesh, from the evil one, or a combination, as some people can start in the Spirit, but wander into the flesh as they prophesy beyond their faith.
- 'To whom have you uttered words? And whose spirit came from you?' (Job 26:4). For warnings and examples of this see: Deuteronomy 13:1-3, 2 Samuel

TAKE HEED? love daddy xxxxx
xx

14:3, 2 Chronicles 18:21-22, Job 32:9, Isaiah 30:1, Jeremiah 14:14, Jeremiah 23:16b, 25-26 and 2 Corinthians 11:4. Jesus warned of false prophets (Matthew 7:15-20, Matthew 24:11, 24 & Luke 6:26), as did the apostles (2 Peter 2:1, 1 John 4:1 & Rev. 16:3).

- 'Having the gifts differing according to the grace that is given us, let us use them; if prophecy, let us prophesy in proportion to our faith' (Romans 12:6).

4. By the mouth of two or three witnesses every word shall be confirmed / established.

- 'This is the third time I am coming to you. 'By the mouth of two or three witnesses every word shall be established' ' (2 Corinthians 13:1).

5. Prophecy is often conditional and we have to fulfill our obligations to our covenant keeping God. If we have not done our part, then we cannot expect God to do His. God will not be mocked by our lifestyles – sins of commission (what we know is wrong) or sins of omission (what we neglect to do) and cannot be cajoled into fulfilling His Word when we have neglected His revealed will as found in the Holy Bible. James stated we should be doers of the Word, and not hearers only, otherwise we deceive ourselves (James 1:22).

- In 2 Chronicles 7:14, in regards to revival, God states, "*If My people* who are called by My name will humble themselves and pray and seek My face, and turn from their wicked ways, *then I will hear* from heaven, and will forgive their sin and heal their land."
- The prophecy from Revelation 1:3 in regards to the Holy Bible needs to be read, heard and kept, and blessed is the person who does this.

'But to each one of us grace was given according to the measure of Christ's gift.... He [Jesus] Himself gave some to be apostles, some prophets, some evangelists, and some pastors and teachers, for the equipping of the saints, for the work of ministry, for the edifying of the Body of Christ [the Church], till we all come to the unity of the faith and the knowledge of the Son of God, to a perfect man, to the measure and stature of the fullness of Christ. That we should no longer be children tossed to and fro and carried about with every wind of doctrine, by the trickery of men, in the cunning craftiness by which they lie in wait to deceive, but speaking the truth in love, may grow up in all things into Him who is the Head – Christ – from whom the whole Body, joined and knit together by what every joint supplies according to the effective working by which every part does its share, cause growth of the Body for the edifying of itself in love' (Ephesians 4:7, 11-16).

Understanding God's Revelations

- 'Surely the Lord God does nothing, unless He reveals His secret to His servants the prophets' (Amos 3:7).
- Hanani the seer said, "For the eyes of the Lord run to and fro throughout the whole earth, to show Himself strong on behalf of those whose heart is loyal to Him..." (2 Chronicles 16:9).
- '...Those who seek the Lord shall not lack any good thing' (Psalm 34:10b).
- 'Delight yourself in the Lord and He shall give you the desires of your heart' (Psalm 37:4).
- 'As the eyes of servants look to the hand of their masters, as the eyes of a maid to the hand of her mistress, so our eyes look to the Lord our God until He has mercy on us' (Psalm 123:2).
- '...Those who seek the Lord understand all' (Proverbs 28:5).
- God said, "For I will pour water on him who is thirsty, and floods on the dry ground; I will pour My Spirit on your descendants, and My blessing on your offspring" (Isaiah 44:3).
- 'Thus says the Lord, the Holy One of Israel, and His Maker, "Ask Me of things to come concerning My sons; and concerning the works of My hands..." ' (Isaiah 45:11).
- Jesus said, "Seek first the Kingdom of God and His righteousness..." (Matthew 6:33).

'This is the Word of the Lord to Zerubbabel, "Not by might nor by power, but by My Spirit," says the Lord of hosts' (Zechariah 4:6).

Chapter 1

Revival – Britain and Ireland (1)

'Thus says the Lord, "For I will pour water on him who is thirsty, and floods on the dry ground; I will pour out My Spirit on your descendants and My blessing on your offspring" ' (Isaiah 44:3).

Great Britain Revival Prophecy (2004)
(A Chain of Grace into Europe)

This is what the Sovereign Lord says,

"For generations the devil has blinded the eyes of the believer and the unbeliever in this nation, to My full sovereign will and the true power of the cross, and the blood of Jesus, My written Word, My commandments, and the Living Bread that came down from Heaven; all this has been hidden from the people of this nation, but this is what the Sovereign Lord says, this is about to change, for in My goodness and My mercy, I shall send a visitation of My power, the power of the Holy Spirit, to turn the hearts of the people away from sin to My Son.

"Millions, yes millions will be saved and swept into My Kingdom, for My glory, and I shall empower them in these last days and they shall fan out as an army of witnesses, sharing the good news, all over this nation, including the islands offshore, and I shall confirm My Word with signs and wonders following them.

"There will be miracles and healings in abundance, and out of this visitation I shall form a chain of grace, that will reach across the Channel into Europe, and to the nations of the world, and there will be a great harvest, an end-time harvest in preparation for Jesus' second coming."

Michael Backholer, 22 March 2004 – www.ProphecyNow.co.uk

This prophecy was proclaimed in June 2004, at the heart of the United Kingdom, Dunsop Bridge, in Lancashire, (near

Lancaster), England. This small village is the exact centre of the United Kingdom and its four hundred and one associated islands, as designated by The Ordinance Survey.

Great Britain Revelation of Revival (2005)

"The blessing of a Heaven-sent revival and end-time outpouring of God's Spirit is backing up like a wall of water offshore. The devil has raised a barrier of unbelief over and around this nation. When the revival prophecy is released, My people will be encouraged by My Spirit and believe, and pray for it to come to pass, and as their faith level rises, so will the sluice gates of unbelief and God's Spirit will flood in with a wave of blessing. This will be followed by wave after wave of liquid love from the Throne of God. Melting the hearts and the minds of the people in all walks of life, from politicians to the homeless, from the elderly to the young, and in the fullness of time the very character of the nation will be changed."

Michael Backholer on Pentecost Sunday, 5 May 2005 – www.ProphecyNow.co.uk

'From the west, men will fear the name of the Lord, and from the rising of the sun, they will revere His glory. For He will come like a pent-up flood that the breath of the Lord drives along' (Isaiah 59:19), NIV.

Upon reflection, the initial floods and huge rivers, which is the initial touch of God will be followed by liquid love to affect the masses over a period of time, perhaps decades or more, which will change the character of the nation.

'O Lord, though our iniquities testify against us, do it for Your name's sake; for our backslidings are many, we have sinned against You' (Jeremiah 14:7).

God said, "By those who come near Me, I must be regarded as holy; and before all the people I must be glorified" (Leviticus 10:3).

Prophecy for Ireland (2005)

This is what the Sovereign Lord says to all of Ireland,

"I have loved you with an everlasting love; I have drawn you with loving-kindness. I have watched over you through troubled times, but now, even now, I am calling you back to My Son. It is He, and He alone that you should put your faith in. He is the One that can truly deliver you, and it was He who died for you, yes all of you; both north and south. And now in these last days, I am calling you back to Myself, come, come I say and drink of that which can truly quench your thirst; not in semi-darkness, but in the true light. Yes, come all of you, enter into and receive the true Light of the World. Do not look to your traditions, look to My Son, Jesus Christ."

Michael Backholer, 12 Nov. 2005 – www.ProphecyNow.co.uk

Prophecy for Wales (2005)

This is what the Sovereign Lord says to Wales,

"Land of valley and song, I say to you again, prepare, prepare for a visitation of My Spirit. I have not forgotten or overlooked you. Once again, the breath of God will be felt as My Spirit bloweth through you; a mighty wind, a powerful wind, a wind of change that will blow the shame from your towns and city centres. Though My back was turned for a time, now is the time for My people to call upon Me in the day of your shame, and I shall turn and deliver you as I have in past generations. And again, voices will be heard all over the valleys, as I breathe a new breath of life into My people, and add greatly to their numbers."

Michael Backholer, 16 Nov. 2005 – www.ProphecyNow.co.uk

Jesus said, "The wind blows where it wishes and you hear the sound of it, but cannot tell where it comes from and where it goes. So is everyone who is born of the Spirit" (John 3:8).

- 14 -

Prophecy for Scotland (2005)

This is what the Sovereign Lord says to Scotland and its islands,

"O Land of the Covenanters, listen to Me, can you not hear My still small voice calling to you from the mountain tops, down the glens and across the lochs? Have you forgotten already when My Spirit came down on the islands in the last generation? Even now, some of My people still cherish in their hearts that time of special visitation, but I give you notice of an even greater visitation that will thunder down from the mountain tops, through the glens and across the lochs. Get ready I say, get ready, this will be a time not to be forgotten; a time of extraordinary blessing.

"If you are to receive all that I have for you at this time – now is the time to make ready; turn from your sin and see My salvation come to the multitudes. Oh yes, I am about to do something so great in your day, that other nations will sit up and take notice. Prepare your hearts and minds to receive all that I shall pour out."

Michael Backholer, 17 Nov. 2005 – www.ProphecyNow.co.uk

Prophecy for England (2005)

This is what the Sovereign Lord says to England,

"In the darkness of your darkest hours you turned to Me, and cried out with one voice, you humbled yourselves and acknowledged your need of Me, and I heard and answered you. When you were in deep despair, you looked to Me to turn the tide and deliver you, and you overcame your enemies.

"You were delivered for a purpose, and yet once again, you took your freedom and went your own way. But now, I am calling you back to finish the work we began together. Your forefathers understood and so must you, there is a Kingdom to be built, one that will last, and I shall call it into being, and you shall rise up again and go forth into My harvest field and proclaim the good news to all the world. Get ready, be prepared, I am about to empower you for My purposes."

Michael Backholer, 18 Nov. 2005 – www.ProphecyNow.co.uk

Prophecy for Great Britain (2006)

This is what the Sovereign Lord says,

"Yes, there is to be a harvest, yes a harvest of souls like no other harvest that this nation has ever experienced. For this harvest is a seed harvest, a harvest that will produce strong healthy seed that can be sent to other nations, that in turn will produce another harvest, and in turn shall be sown again and again. The wind of My Spirit shall blow the seed all over the earth in every direction and it shall germinate and grow, and spread forth its fruit, and there will be fields with sheaves in every nation. That which was foretold from the beginning shall come to pass, and the sower and the reaper shall work hand in hand and be led by My Spirit to the most fertile places on this earth, as well as the dry and arid places. Yes, this will be a harvest to end all harvests. The Spirit of the Lord has spoken and it shall come to pass."

Michael Backholer, 16 Jan. 2006 – www.ProphecyNow.co.uk

To the British Isles – A New Day Dawns
(Light will Penetrate Every Area of Your Kingdom)

This is what the Sovereign Lord says to the British Isles,

"I am the Light of the World, and My light is about to break forth and penetrate the darkness and shine brighter than the noonday sun and dispel the darkness all over this nation. At times it will come with such ferocity, it will be as a consuming fire that will burn and scorch all in its path, and all that is dross shall be removed.

"My light will penetrate every area of your kingdom and be transformed into My Kingdom by the power of the blood of

Jesus Christ, and the light of the gospel of truth will flood back into your communities to cleanse and restore all that the thief came to steal, kill and destroy. And again, this shall indeed be a green and pleasant land, a land to sing about. But this is only the beginning, because as My Spirit sanctifies all that is born anew, so shall I raise up men and women with a social conscience who will labour night and day to restore this nation, and in the fullness of time you shall indeed be called 'Great' as this was, and still is, your destiny as a nation."

Michael Backholer, 3 Sept. 2006 – www.ProphecyNow.co.uk

The Promised Revival – Great Britain

This is what the Sovereign Lord says,

"Some of you say, 'We have watched and waited and still we see no sign of the promised revival,' and I say to you, did not Elijah send his servant to look towards the sea and he said, 'There is nothing.' Seven times he was obedient to his master and returned and looked, until he saw a small cloud, no bigger than a man's hand.

"In Africa after long periods without rain, some can smell and taste the coming rain long before they see it. The wind of change is coming to Great Britain, you may not see the wind, but listen and you will hear it, and in the fullness of time you will feel the breeze. But this calls for faith and trust. Faith is being sure of what we hope for and certain of what we do not see. So I say to you, look up, cheer up and be encouraged, for I do nothing without revealing My plans to My servants the prophets. That is why Elijah could say to his servant, 'Go back.' So I say to you, pray on, be watchful, be alert, keep looking, don't give up and your faith will be rewarded in full.

"The gentle breeze is blowing from the north and in the fullness of time it will blow stronger and stronger until it reaches gale force, and My Spirit shall be poured out from on high, and there shall be a drenching, and in places a deluge, and the world will watch in wonder."

Michael Backholer, 2 Dec. 2006 – www.ProphecyNow.co.uk

Judgment and Revival
(Great Britain Ablaze)

This is what the Sovereign Lord says,

"To the faithful few, the praying remnant who have stood before Me in the gap on behalf of Great Britain and interceded, believing that judgment was imminent. You have cried out to Me for mercy, time and time again, up and down this once great nation, and I have heard the cry of your hearts and for that reason, My goodness and My mercy shall prevail.

"Judgment has begun at the house of the Lord and it is necessary, but I have not finished with Great Britain as some suppose. So in My goodness and My mercy, I shall again revive My Church and then set the nation ablaze. Out of this great fire will emerge disciples who will be red-hot and on fire for My name, and as they walk through the fields that are ready for harvest, more fires will ignite and breakout; and the smoke shall rise as a pillar of cloud for all to see as a witness to the peoples of the world. Then will be the time for judgment, but it will be in My way and in My time, for I am the Beginning and the End."

Michael Backholer, 6 Dec. 2006 – www.ProphecyNow.co.uk

Revival is a two-edged sword – a blessing for many and judgment for a minority. It is 'a sign that is spoken against' for 'the fall and rising of many' because God's presence will reveal the true state of people's hearts (Luke 2:35). The blessing of revival is to cut free and deliver, for the cleansing, purging, sifting, shaking and restoration of the Church, '...do not despise the chastening of the Almighty. For He bruises, but He binds up; He wounds, but His hands make whole' (Job 5:17-18). Be warned, the judgment of revival is for a minority of the Body of Christ who are unrepentant and wilfully living in habitual sin, those who continually dishonour the name of the Lord, because judgment always begins at the house of the Lord (1 Peter 4:17, c.f. Ezekiel 9:6 and Acts 8:18-24). See also Psalm 73:18, Isaiah 66:15-16, Nahum 1:6, 9-10, and Acts 12:1-12.

Some Christians are pessimists of revival believing, "It is not for today," but is this biblical? The Scriptures declare otherwise. God says, "I will pour out My Spirit..." (Joel 2:28a) and the work of the Holy Spirit still continues. The 'promise of the Father' is still available (Acts 1:4), and we must all receive our own Pentecost, power for victorious Christian living (Acts 1:8). Lord, send revival, but start the work in me!

God said, "If My people who are called by My name will humble themselves, and pray and seek My face, and turn from their wicked ways, then I will hear from heaven, and will forgive their sin and heal their land" (2 Chronicles 7:14).

God said, "For I will pour water on him who is thirsty, and floods on the dry ground; I will pour out My Spirit on your descendants and My blessing on your offspring" (Isaiah 44:3).

Thus says the Lord, "Rain down, you heavens, from above, and let the skies pour down righteousness; let the earth open, let them bring forth salvation, and let righteousness spring up together. I the Lord have created it" (Isaiah 45:8).

'Oh, that You would rend the Heavens and come down! That the mountains might shake at Your presence...to make Your name known' (Isaiah 64:1).

Some Christians are fed up with talk of revival, but God is broken-hearted that many don't want it – just look at the Church (with it sins of commission and omission) and then at society (how it is broken, does not fear God and has ungodly laws)!

Many Christians say that revival is "not for today," yet the Scriptures, Church history and the revivalists all disprove this! What Bible did Jonathan Edwards, the Wesley's, George Whitefield, Charles Finney, Charles Spurgeon, D. L. Moody, Jonathan Goforth, Evan Roberts, William Seymour, Smith Wigglesworth, J. Edwin Orr and Duncan Campbell have? They had the same Bible / Scriptures to plead and obey as we have today! They lived up to God's standards, knew how to plead the promises contained within the Bible and saw the heavenly fire fall! God was glorified, Jesus was exalted and the Holy Spirit was given His rightful place within the Church. Saints were revived, sinners were saved and backsliders were brought back into the fold of God. Fruit was born in people's lives and the Kingdom of God advanced! See *Revival Answers*, and *Revival Fires and Awakenings*, both by Mathew Backholer.

Chapter 2

Revival – Britain and Ireland (2)

The Lord said, "If My people who are called by My name will humble themselves, and pray and seek My face, and turn from their wicked ways, then I will hear from heaven, and will forgive their sin and heal their land" (2 Chronicles 7:14).

A Call to Prayer for the United Kingdom and Ireland (The Coming Revival – 7-7-7)

This is what the Sovereign Lord says,

"To My people who are called by My name in the United Kingdom of Great Britain, and Ireland. A great change has taken place over these islands, so now I am calling you by My Spirit to humble yourselves and pray; to build up the wall and stand in the gap on behalf of the land and turn from your wicked ways. Then will I hear from Heaven and forgive your sin, and heal your land for My glory.

"I would remind you of what I said through My servants Smith Wigglesworth, shortly before I called him home, and all that I said through Jean Darnall;[1] that these nations and indeed the rest of the world would witness the greatest move of My Spirit that these islands have ever seen. A revival, an awakening that will eclipse anything that has gone before. This will come at great cost to some, but like those who went before, they shall say, it was worth it.

"I am calling for unity of Spirit, as you call out to Me with one voice. I shall open the floodgates of Heaven and all that Joel and Peter spoke of shall come to pass for My glory. I shall pour out My Spirit on all flesh; every level of society and people group will witness My power.

"Many of the people from other nations who have come here will be transformed by My Spirit to the surprise of many and will return to their own homelands to share the good news of the gospel of Jesus Christ, the Messiah."

Michael Backholer, 7 July 2007 (07-07-07) – www.ProphecyNow.co.uk

1. For their prophecy and vision see: www.RevivalNow.co.uk.

The Glowing Coals of Faith in Wales
(Will Breakout in Revival Fires)

This is what the Sovereign Lord says,

"Shortly after the turn of the last century there was a Divine stirring in Wales as the hand of God began to stir the cinders and shake the ashes of a bygone fire. And in the fullness of time Wales was once again ablaze, as flames of revival swept through valleys and over mountains. So great was that fire that others came to carry a burning coal back to their nations which in turn ignited other fires.

"But it was not long before the enemy who seeks to destroy the work I do by My Spirit, began to dig a pit which many in Wales fell into. And furthermore, over the years as the coal pits closed, so the fire died down, and a new generation was born whose eyes have been blinded by the god of this age, who hid from them their true inheritance.

"But there is a remnant who did not forget, and I have called them to Wales, to bring their glowing coals of faith to join with the remnant in Wales. And again there is a stirring as I begin to blow again upon these embers that have come together and fires will again breakout all over Wales, and as they grow bigger and stronger so shall they become one fire that shall burn with such ferociousness that the demonic will flee from it as their strongholds are torn down.

"And once again, white gloves will be given out as a sign of My power and holiness, which destroys all the works of Satan. And again flaming coals will be taken to other nations to prepare for My Kingdom to come and My will be done, here on earth, as it is in Heaven. And voices shall be raised in glad adoration as the Bread of Heaven is again sung with all its true meaning, which will reverberate round the stadiums for My everlasting glory."

Michael Backholer, 21 July 2007 – www.ProphecyNow.co.uk

To the United Kingdom of Great Britain
(Do you Truly Believe?)

This is what the Sovereign Lord says,

"To all those in the United Kingdom of Great Britain: from the Shetland Islands to the Isles of Scilly, to the Channel Islands – all who believe in Jesus. What do you believe? Who do you say I am? Do you truly believe I am the Christ, the Son of the Living God? Do you truly believe all that is written in the Holy Scriptures about Me? Do you defend My name in your town and marketplace or have you remained silent in your belief? Or perhaps even embarrassed for fear of how others might react to you.

"When the Holy Spirit came at Pentecost, My disciples were empowered from on high and spoke in tongues, and went out and lifted up My name, which is above every other name for all to hear. And the people cried out, 'What must we do to be saved?' and I confirmed their message with miraculous signs and wonders, and their world was turned upside down.

"They had spent much time in prayer, seeking My presence and My power, so I say to you, confess your need for My presence and My power and be ready for what I am about to do in your nation for all the world to see. I have been preparing My Church for such a time as this when My Spirit shall be poured out to the full, all over the nation for My glory. And I shall do even greater things than you could ever believe or imagine.

"But, be warned, My Spirit will not strive with you, should you resist Him and cling on to the traditions of your forefathers. You must choose your will or Mine, for many have denied or avoided the work of My Spirit and if you continue to do so, I shall pass you by. So do not oppose this end-time move of My Spirit, as many have in the past to their own detriment and to the eternal detriment of others."

Michael Backholer, 2 August 2007 – www.ProphecyNow.co.uk

God gives the Holy Spirit to those who obey Him – not the disobedient (Acts 5:32). Your Heavenly Father will give the Holy Spirit to those who ask – have you? (Luke 11:13).

To the United Kingdom of Great Britain
(A Spiritual Tsunami)

This is what the Sovereign Lord says to the United Kingdom of Great Britain,

"The first stage of a spiritual tsunami has taken place in and around your shores stretching deep within the very fabric of your island / islands. The true power of My presence withdrew like the tide withdraws in the Bristol Channel from Weston-Super-Mare. But as sure as night follows day, in the fullness of time the tide turns and returns to wash away man's footprints in the sand. So shall the power of My presence return to your shores as you humble yourselves, and pray and seek My face and turn from your wicked ways; like the waves of a tsunami flooding deep inland. Once again, the power of the Holy Spirit will flood in and drive out the powers of darkness that have choked out the light, and the life of My Word from this once great nation.

"Your Empire did not last a thousand years and your finest hours are still to come. There is a work to be completed in you and the nations of the world that only My Holy Spirit can achieve. Jesus spoke of it and John recorded it in his Gospel.

"The watchmen are on the ramparts watching the harvest ripen. Make ready the harvesters, sharpen your sickles and reaping hooks, and watch in amazement as I bring forth My combine harvesters. So make ready your barns and your silos for such a time as this."

Michael Backholer, 15 Sept. 2007 – www.ProphecyNow.co.uk

It has been estimated that every hour 7,000 people who did not trust in Jesus Christ as their Lord and Saviour, die and go to Hell. Whilst we believe and pray for revival, we are commanded to go into all the world and make disciples of all the nations and then the end will come (Matthew 24:14 and 2 Peter 3:12). We must go into the highways and byways, and compel people to come in. We must be obedient to the Great Commission of which Jesus spoke about (Matthew 28:18-20, Mark 16:15-18, Luke 24:47 and Acts 1:8).

To Great Britain
(The Land of Hope and Glory)

This is what the Sovereign Lord says to Great Britain,

"Many have heard, sung, whistled or hummed along to the tune of 'Land of Hope and Glory,' but few have really understood the words of introduction. Hope is the expectation of something truly desired deep within one's own heart, which calls for faith. Faith is being sure of what we hope for and certain of what we do not see. The glory is mine; I will not give to or share it with another. But when My glory descends in all its majesty; men and women alike drop to their knees in awe or are prostrated, overcome in all submissiveness.

"Look, watch and be amazed, for I am going to do something in Great Britain, in your days that most would not believe, even if they were told. For I shall again visit this nation for My glory, due in part, in answer to the prayers of millions. Yes, millions of children who prayed daily:

" 'Our Father which art in Heaven, hallowed be Thy name. Thy Kingdom come, Thy will be done on earth, as it is in Heaven. Give us this day our daily bread and forgive us our debts, as we forgive our debtors and lead us not into temptation, but deliver us from evil. For Thine is the Kingdom and the power and the glory, for ever. Amen.'

"I have not forgotten, did you?"

Michael Backholer, 28 Oct. 2007 – www.ProphecyNow.co.uk

After camping at Elim, the Israelites moved to the Wilderness of Sin. Aaron spoke to Israelite congregation and as 'they looked towards the wilderness, and behold, the glory of the Lord appeared in the cloud' (Exodus 16:10).

'Tell your children about it, let your children tell their children, and their children another generation' (Joel 1:3).

'Our God shall come...' (Psalm 50:3).

Two Weddings and a Double-Minded Spirit
(Saying One Thing and Doing Another)

This is what the Sovereign Lord says,

"Billions, yes billions watched a Christian religious ceremony and rejoiced, and celebrated long into the night. People slept on the streets in order to get a good view, and the world's press was caught up in it for a season. A man and a woman came into God's house to make a covenant agreement to each other, and to a covenant keeping God. Silver trumpets sounded out in-keeping with the Word of God, at times of rejoicing. A blessing was pronounced in and through the name of the Lord and Saviour Jesus Christ. A seed of eternal life was requested to be sown in the couple's heart, so that they should inherit the everlasting Kingdom.

"There was a lesson on presenting their bodies as a living sacrifice, holy and acceptable to God. There was singing about building a new Jerusalem in England for the Holy Lamb of God. The congregation prayed for God's Kingdom to come, and His will to be done here as in Heaven. The choir declared in song that this was the day that the Lord had made, and that they should rejoice and be glad. The people cheered as the couple passed by them in their coach, drawn by white horses with riders. Little knowing that one day, they would face another Rider of a white horse who is called Faithful and True. It was declared a joyful day, a day of hope. The couple had composed a prayer and made their vows.[2]

"Sadly says the Lord in this day, in this hour, with the passing of time, for many, words come cheap. Hollow words from hollow hearts, and vows broken which breaks hearts. Beware I say, beware a double-minded spirit has taken root when you say one thing and do another. Time flies by like the Lancaster, Hurricane and Spitfire, but your vows to God are everlasting and written in stone. Blessed are those who are invited to the wedding supper of the Lamb."

Michael Backholer, 1 May 2011 – www.ProphecyNow.co.uk

2. On Friday 29 April 2011, Prince William and Catherine "Kate" Middleton married at Westminster Abbey, London, England.

The Game of Shame
(I have Removed Many things from you as a Nation)

This is what the Sovereign Lord says,

"Wave the flag, blow the whistle, show them the yellow card. Wave the flag it's a foul, it's a foul, wave the flag. Foul I say, foul, wave the flag. Show the red card, blow the whistle, send them off, book them, send them off. The Premier League has sown the wind and will reap the whirlwind, says the Lord. There are stadiums sinking, yes sinking I say, going down like the Titanic. No, no they say this will never happen, they are unsinkable. No, says the Lord God, some will sink under the weight and burden of debt, their wheeling and dealing, and stealing is like an iceberg.

"When a nation under God with an empire turns its back on the apple of God's eye, and turns away and rejects the very foundations that made it great, and gives its affections to another and other things, they also reject My blessing, says the Lord, when millions every weekend give their love and affection to others, remember I warned you not to make an idol of another or worship them. The Lord your God is a jealous God and punishes the children of the fathers to the third and fourth generation of those who hate Him, but shows love to a thousand generations who love Him and keep His commandments.

"I have removed many things from you as a nation hoping that you would turn from your wicked ways and give Me your attention. But still, you are unmoved, says the Lord God but know this, when the thing that you love and support with all your heart, soul and strength is demoted and dethroned in financial collapse, you are reaping what you sowed.

"Do not weep over empty stadiums, but repent, for I shall surely fill them when I pour out My Spirit on all flesh, and again you will hear a screaming roar from an own goal, for you have reaped what you have sown and are way offside, and the roar and the screaming will be the demonic spirits being cast out in Jesus' name. I am the Alpha and the Omega and I am calling the shots for I AM Sovereign. Time is running out, and I am calling full time I shall blow the whistle so repent while there is still time, or pay the penalty."

Michael Backholer, 8 May 2011 – www.ProphecyNow.co.uk

- 'Who may ascend into the hill of the Lord? Or who may stand in His holy place? He who has clean hands and a pure heart, who has not lifted up his soul to an idol, nor sworn deceitfully. He shall receive blessing from the Lord and righteousness from the God of his salvation. This is Jacob, the generation of those who seek Him...' (Psalm 24:3-6). See also Psalm 15.
- 'Sow for yourselves righteousness; reap in mercy; break up your fallow ground, for it is time to seek the Lord, till He comes and rains righteousness on you' (Hosea 10:12).
- 'I acknowledged my sin to You and my iniquity I have not hidden. I said, "I will confess my transgression to the Lord," and You forgave the iniquity of my sin. Selah. For this cause everyone who is godly will pray to You' (Psalm 32:5-6a).
- 'If I regard iniquity in my heart, the Lord will not hear' (Psalm 66:18). See also Isaiah 59:2 and John 9:31.
- 'One who turns away his ear from hearing the law, even his prayer shall be an abomination' (Proverbs 28:9).
- 'Let us search out and examine our ways, and turn back to the Lord; let us lift up our hearts and hands to God in Heaven. We have transgressed and rebelled.... You have covered Yourself with a cloud that prayer should not pass through' (Lamentations 3:40-42a, 44). See Ps. 139:23-24.
- 'He who covers his sins will not prosper. But whoever confesses and forsakes them will find mercy' (Proverbs 28:13). See also Leviticus 5:5, Acts 19:18 and James 5:16.
- Does our heart condemn us? Is our conscience pricked with unconfessed sin, because we have not kept God's commandments and therefore, we are not pleasing in His sight? (1 John 3:21-22).
- Confessions of our sins, the sins of our forefathers and our nation's sins are paramount (Exodus 20:5-6, Judges 2:6-19 and 1 John 1:9). We need to make sure that we are right before God. Unless we deal with the sins of the past it is impossible to move forward into *all* that God wants for us.

Chapter 3

Great Britain and Other Nations

Jesus said, "Whoever confesses Me before men, him I will also confess before My Father who is in Heaven. But whoever denies Me before men, him I will also deny before My Father who is in Heaven. Do not think that I came to bring peace on earth. I did not come to bring peace, but a sword. For I have come to 'set a man against his father, a daughter against her mother, and a daughter-in-law against her mother-in-law,' and 'a man's foes will be those of his own household.' He who loves father or mother more than Me is not worthy of Me, and he who loves son or daughter more than Me is not worthy of Me" (Matthew 10:32-37).

Prophecy for Great Britain and Other Nations
(My Sword will Again Pass Through this Land)

This is what the Sovereign Lord says,

"My sword will again pass through this land and you shall see a distinct separation between that which is righteous and that which is not. And indeed My Word which is My sword will pass not only through this land, but through many other nations as well. And you shall see it pass through people groups and families as well as My Body, the Body of Christ. And you shall see a separation and understand that which is written in My Word, that on that day, many, yes, many who profess Me as Lord shall say, 'Lord, Lord, did we not do all this in Your name?' And I shall tell them plainly, I know you not. So keep watch because all that is written shall come to pass, and I shall return for a spotless, pure and holy Bride. The voice of the Lord has spoken. Keep watch I say, keep watch, for the days are indeed dark, but I am the Light of the World and I shall shine for all to see, and those who truly walk in My light shall be saved, and those who refuse My light shall perish."

Michael Backholer, 24 Jan. 2006 – www.ProphecyNow.co.uk

To the Nations of the World
(Abortion – Killing Unborn Children)

This is what the Sovereign Lord says,

"Did you ever truly stop to consider what effect your decision to kill unborn children while still in their mothers' wombs would have on your societies as a whole? Did you truly think I would not notice, or did you not even care? But I did notice, I saw it all, and I call it mass murder of babies that were created by Myself. Were you not all horrified when you learnt what was done in Satan's name, during what you have called the Second World War? And so I ask you, in whose name did you decide on this wholesale slaughter of the innocent while still inside their mothers' wombs; in which I placed a spirit within every body. Consider then, if you dare, where their spirits went to when you destroyed their bodies, that I knitted together in their mothers' wombs in which they were closeted. And why was it designed the way it is? I shall tell you, it was designed that way to protect the unborn child, yes that's right, an unborn child. Furthermore, it was designed as a place of safety and yet you have made it one of the most dangerous places for a baby to be. Have you forgotten or did you choose to forget that down the ages, how mothers' hid their babies from Satan's hatred of mankind and his murderous hordes? Now, in the closing stages of this age, I call all nations to repent, for the blood of your children calls out to Me from the very ground you stand on." [Genesis 4:10].

Michael Backholer, 20 Feb. 2006 – www.ProphecyNow.co.uk

- "Your eyes saw my substances, being yet unformed. And in Your Book they were all written, the days fashioned for me, when as yet there were none of them" (Psalm 139:16).
- God said to Jeremiah, "Before I formed you in the womb I knew you, before you were born I sanctified you and I ordained you a prophet to the nations" (Jeremiah 1:5).
- 'It pleased God who separated me from my mother's womb and called me through His grace, to reveal His Son in me, that I might preach among the Gentiles...' (Gal. 1:15-16).

Orphans and Spiritual Fathers of Great Britain
(George Müller)

This is what the Sovereign Lord says,

"I have said that I will not leave you as orphans; I will come to you. Now in this generation there is an overwhelming need in Great Britain for spiritual fathers, when so many are lost and destitute, morally and spiritually. "As My servant, George Müller[1] was a father to the orphans of Bristol, so shall I be a Father by My Spirit to all who reach out to Me with a heartfelt need. Then I shall raise them up and clothe them with My Spirit, so their faces shall reflect My glory as I transform them into My likeness, and they shall be My ambassadors whom I will send out among the peoples of the earth with the good news.

"I shall reach out to others in need through them, and as surely as the earth will be filled with the knowledge of the glory of the Lord as the waters cover the sea, so shall they spread out to reflect My glory for all to see. First in Great Britain, then to the nations of the world, and I shall equip them and arm them with My Word, power, and faith, to reach others who are fatherless."

Michael Backholer, 1 January 2007 – www.ProphecyNow.co.uk

1. In 1833, George Müller (1805-1898) founded an orphanage in Bristol, England, supported by prayer and faith in the living God. In 1849, the Ashley Down orphanage was built and at the height of his ministry, George Müller looked after 2,000 orphans!

The apostle Paul wrote to the young Church at Thessalonica, 'But we were gentle among you, just as a nursing mother cherishes her own children. So affectionately longing for you, we were well pleased to impart to you, not only the gospel of God, but also our own lives, because you had become dear to us.... As you know how we exhorted and comforted, and charged every one of you, as a father does his own children, that you would have a walk worthy of God, who calls you into His own Kingdom and glory' (1 Thessalonians 2:7-8, 11-12).

Chapter 4

For the Body of Christ – The Church

'Gird yourselves and lament you priests; wail, you who minister before the altar, come lie all night in sackcloth you who minister to my God' (Joel 1:13).

A Word for the Body of Christ
(Spiritual Fathers of your Generation)

This is what the Sovereign Lord says,

"To those who are truly alert, watching and waiting at the door, you will have noticed that many of the spiritual fathers of your generation have departed from among you. Be encouraged I say, for I am raising up new fathers that the hearts and minds of My children will turn to. They have already gone ahead of you to prepare the way like John did for Me. When you hear their voices, listen to them for they have seen the pitfalls and the dangers that lie ahead. But also, they have experienced them and will warn you of the same. Yes, indeed you are a most privileged generation, but there is a cost and a cross to bear daily; be of good cheer for I have overcome and so shall you. Draw near to Me and I shall draw near to you.

"Test all things in this hour against My Word, for I have said, 'You shall know them by their fruit.' Look for the fruit and you need not be deceived; for there will be false prophets and tares among you, and in places you did not expect to find them, so be on your guard at all times."

Michael Backholer, 25 Jan. 2006 – www.ProphecyNow.co.uk

The apostle Paul wrote: '...As my beloved children, I warn you. For though you might have ten thousand instructors in Christ, yet you do not have many fathers: for in Christ Jesus I have begotten you through the gospel. Therefore I urge you, to imitate me' (1 Corinthians 4:14-16).

Wake Up, Wake Up
(Warfare – Riots or Revival)

This is what the Sovereign Lord says,

"Wake up, wake up, I say, the Spirit is willing, but the flesh is weak, this is not the time to sleep or slumber. Wake up, I say, the days of darkness are upon you and still you sleep. Let those who have ears hear what the Spirit says to the Church; open your eyes, open your ears, open your mouths. Now is the time to call upon the Lord, and those who call upon the Lord shall be delivered. I will not do battle alone, you have your part to play. I call My Body, yes My Body, to take hold of your weapons of warfare and do battle. The enemy is not at the door, he has entered the abode, open your eyes and look; how could you not see? Listen to Me, the enemy has blinded the eyes of the believer as well as the unbeliever, to what he is up to. Samson awoke when it was too late, do not let the same happen to you. Now is the hour to gird up your loins, pick up your sword and shield and do battle, you fight not with flesh and blood. You have a choice: either riots or revival. These can indeed be the most glorious days of My Church; if My people, who are called by My name, will humble themselves and pray, and seek My face, and turn from their wicked ways, then will I hear from Heaven and will forgive their sin and will heal their land. This is My covenant promise to every nation under the Son. Have I not said that in the last days, all that is written will come to pass, and is it not written that as sin abounds, more so shall My grace abound. Don't hide your lamps under a table; stand up for what you believe. What are you waiting for!"

Michael Backholer, 22 Feb. 2006 – www.ProphecyNow.co.uk

'Turn to Me with all your heart, with fasting, with weeping, and with mourning. So rend your heart, and not your garments; return to the Lord your God; for He is gracious and merciful, slow to anger, and of great kindness, and He relents from doing harm' (Joel 2:12-13).

To the World-Loving Lukewarm Churches
(Repent While there is Still Time)

This is what the Sovereign Lord says,

"To the world-loving lukewarm churches, I AM the One with the sharp double-edged sword, and I shall return with My angels to separate the sheep from the goats. Do you not know that bad company corrupts good character? So come out and be separate while there is still time. For there is coming upon the earth an hour of trial and testing like nothing that the earth has experienced before. But you are not ready, even now your hands are dirty, and your hearts are far from pure.

"I get no pleasure in the death of the wicked, but much prefer that they turn from their wicked ways. So I say, consider carefully the height from which you have fallen and repent while there is still time. Do not be fooled into thinking that another two thousand years will pass before My return. Look at the fig tree, it shall soon bear fruit and it is fruit I am looking for, and if I do not find it, beware, or you to may find yourself withering from the roots up. Let those who have ears to hear what the Spirit says to the Church. Oh, how foolish some of you are, thinking that you could continue with your traditions and rules taught by men, leaving My Holy Spirit to knock on your doors; repent I say, repent while there is still time."

Michael Backholer, 7 March 2006 – www.ProphecyNow.co.uk

It is the 'Lord [who] kills and makes alive; He brings down to the grave and brings up...He brings low and lifts up' (1 Samuel 2:6-7). The Scriptures declare: 'Utterly slay...begin at My sanctuary' (Ezekiel 9:6). 'Blow the trumpet in Zion...tremble; for the day of the Lord is coming' (Joel 2:1). God said, "I will come to you quickly and remove your lampstand from its place – unless you repent" (Revelation 2:5). God's righteous judgment must come (Ezekiel 9:6, James 4:5 and 1 Peter 4:17-18) and He does retire individuals and shuts churches! See 1 Corinthians 11:27-31, 2 Thessalonians 1:8-9 and Revelation chapters 1-3.

Careless Words and Choreographed Preachers
(Access to the Power of the Media and its Abuse)

This is what the Sovereign Lord says,

"I would remind you of that which is written in My Word, that on the day of judgment everyone, yes, everyone will have to give an account for every careless word they have said. Furthermore, by those very same words they will be acquitted or condemned. I would draw your attention to the fact that words come cheap, very cheap indeed, so cheap that you scatter them around like confetti, especially when you say, 'The Lord says,' but did I? Or, 'I prophesy,' indeed you did, but whose spirit spoke out of your mouth? For many speak out of the imaginations of their own minds, and did you really think that by shouting that you could project an illusion of My anointing? Come now, let us show some degree of reason to this matter. It has not gone unnoticed by My people that some of you with access to the power of the media use the spoken word like a parrot. You copy each other instead of being the servant I called you to be. You choreograph every move in your all singing, all dancing act. Now! Now, I call you to examine your ways long and hard because as we enter into the final act of this age, I do not wish to see an encore. You will indeed be called to give an account for every performance of your playacting and you will reap what you have sown."

Michael Backholer, 11 March 2006 – www.ProphecyNow.co.uk

You are Without Excuse – I shall Leave no Stone Unturned
(The Love of Many has Grown Cold)

This is what the Sovereign Lord says to His Church,

"In the closing hours of this dispensation I have to say to My Church, you are without excuse. All that happened in the past was written down as an example and as a warning for you on whom the fulfilment of this age has come.

"My judgment, yes My judgment has already begun and it starts with you. I shall leave no stone unturned and look behind every bush, and all that can be sifted and shaken shall be. Be warned, this will truly be an uncomfortable time for many, but it is necessary to purify My Bride from all unrighteousness in readiness for the marriage supper.

"I have much to say to you about the state of your hearts and minds. I have suffered, yes suffered and tolerated much, but no longer will I put up with your unclean hands and impure hearts. Many of you have prostituted yourselves and committed spiritual adultery in every way imaginable, and I refuse to tolerate that kind of unfaithfulness any longer. You are without excuse. Now is the time to confess your sins one to another and repent, and turn from your sinful lifestyles.

"It is also written in what manner you should conduct yourselves when you eat and drink at My table in remembrance of Me, and yet many, yes many, still partake in an unworthy way. Is it any wonder so many of you are sick and some have fallen asleep prematurely.

"You have had fair warning, now is the time to turn away from all that is superficial and meaningless and spend time with My Word and in My presence. To many of you, I am no more than a stranger, yet you cry out to Me in times of trouble, and believe Me, troubled times are coming as well as blessed times. For some, it shall indeed be a special time of blessing, but for others troubled times, as you reap what you have sown.

"The love of many has already grown cold and more will follow. Let those who have ears hear; open your eyes wide and you will see a true and an apostate Church. You have been warned. Be alert, for some are preaching another Jesus and a different gospel with another spirit. Consider carefully what you hear, with the measure you have used, with that same measure you will receive."

Michael Backholer, 27 March 2006 – www.ProphecyNow.co.uk

'Blow the trumpet in Zion, consecrate a fast, call a sacred assembly; gather the people, sanctify the congregation, assemble the elders, gather the children and the nursing babes …Let the priests, who minister to the Lord weep between the porch and the altar…' (Joel 2:15-17).

Chapter 5

America and Europe

'For the Lord Himself will descend from Heaven with a shout, with the voice of an archangel, and with the trumpet of God. And the dead in Christ will rise first. Then we who are alive and remain shall be caught up in the clouds to meet the Lord in the air. And thus we shall always be with the Lord' (1 Thess. 4:16).

To My Shepherds in the United States of America, Great Britain and Europe (Go and Make Disciples of all Nations)

This is what the Sovereign Lord says,

"To My shepherds, do you not say, before the darkest hour is the dawn? Yes, these are indeed dark days and that darkness shall become even darker, but do not concern yourself too much with that. Rejoice I say, rejoice, for did I not say it would be so? Rejoice I say, rejoice, as it gets darker and it will, so shall My light shine brighter.

"Do you truly understand the days you are living in? Are you looking for My return? Some are; there is a remnant who are preparing and teaching My people in preparation for that day – what about you? Have I not said, prepare My people for works of service? Did you not understand that you were to be about My Father's business, building His Kingdom? And what about My sheep that are scattered; have you searched for them? And the hurt ones, have you bandaged their wounds? And have you healed the sick ones, or were you too busy doing what you thought should be done? Not many of you find the time to sit at My feet as Mary did; you are part of the Martha generation – always keeping busy, so busy you don't hear what I am saying. And what of My new born lambs who skip and jump, who look to you to teach and train them how to do what My disciples did, and still do. Do you truly understand what I am saying? Go and make *disciples* of all nations. My sheep look to you week after week and you say everything you need is in God's Word, and rightly so. However, there are large portions you yourselves have turned a blind eye to; so much so, that some are walking out of balance and walk round in circles, never really getting to the full truth. Now is the time to make the time and seek Me with all your being, and give the Holy Spirit His rightful place in My Father's house. Then you can truly say, Jesus is among us, and furthermore, you shall witness that I AM truly the same yesterday, and today and forever."

Michael Backholer, 26 Feb. 2006 – www.ProphecyNow.co.uk

Jesus said, "All authority has been given to Me in Heaven and on earth. Go therefore and make disciples of all the nations, baptising them in the name of the Father and of the Son and of the Holy Spirit, teaching them to observe all things that I have commanded you; and lo, I am with you always, even to the end of the age" (Matthew 28:18-20).

United States of America, Great Britain and Europe
(Prepare your Nets – Make Ready)

This is what the Sovereign Lord says,

"To My faithful ones, those who have laboured all night and caught little or nothing, I say, prepare your nets, yes that's right, prepare your nets! Get ready, in a little while the River of God will be in full flood. You must be ready to put out into the deep water and let down your nets. Did I not say that I would make you fishers of men? So make ready, your nets must be made strong. And I tell you now that you will require many helpers to land the catch that I have for you. Make ready and consider carefully what you will do with the catch. I do not want anything wasted; remember when I fed the multitude with the bread and the fish? Nothing, nothing I say was wasted and likewise I expect you to do the same. It will be harvest time again, prepare I say, prepare, you don't have long to get ready; the fields are white unto harvest. Oh, what a season this will be, a much greater harvest than you could have ever imagined, but you must make ready. Joseph knew that when the harvest was plentiful, preparations had to be made. Think long and hard about this, I can send a harvest, but you are responsible for it. What will you do with so much coming so quickly? Think about these things, sit down with others and talk and pray about such things. When I told My disciples to go and make preparations in the upper room, they did so. Later I told them to wait in Jerusalem for the gift My Father had promised and so they did as I told them. So I say again, make preparations for I am about to pour out My Spirit like never before. Believe Me when I say, this is not a time for doom and gloom, this is a time to rejoice, so make ready, make sure everything, yes, everything is in its place to receive and process the harvest."

Michael Backholer, 27 Feb. 2006 – www.ProphecyNow.co.uk

'Those who sow in tears shall reap in joy. He who continually goes forth weeping, bearing seed for sowing, shall doubtless come again with rejoicing, bringing his sheaves with him' (Psalm 126:5-6).

The Latter-Day Outpouring of My Spirit
(To America and Great Britain)

This is what the Sovereign Lord says to America and Great Britain,

"Many believe that I have turned away from you, as you turned away from Me, but this is untrue. Others choose to believe that this is their time and they can seduce you to slip and slide further into darkness, and follow the teachings of one of the most dogmatic ideologies known to man with its cruel barbaric ways. They have no understanding whatsoever of My love, mercy, grace and compassion for all of mankind.
"Even though you have brought great shame and disgrace on My name for all the world to see, and you have been unfaithful in the extreme and prostituted yourselves in My sight. Even so, I shall have compassion on you for My own name's sake and for the sake of the watchmen who I called, and were obedient to stand on your ramparts, and cry out to Me day and night to stay My hand on your behalf.

"Nothing is too difficult or impossible for Me. Can a nation be born in a day? Can a people who were scattered all over the earth be reunited to its centre?[1] Can a nation given over to voodoo and witchcraft be humbled in a moment of time?[2] There is no wall, iron curtain, or bamboo blind that can stand in My way. When I choose to pour out My Spirit on a people group or nation, the greater their sin, the greater the glory when they repent and turn to Me through My Son.

"Wales is known by some as 'The Land of Revivals,' but did you notice the outpouring today [Friday 1 October 2010] in Wales at the Ryder Cup competition? There was a deluge, and a drenching, even the Tiger sheltered under wood. This was autumn rain that man could shelter from; even so, the Americans and others discovered that their waterproofs were inadequate in this downpour. This was just a small taste of what is to come with the latter-day outpouring of My Spirit on America, Britain and Europe.

"Many who through fear have lived under one of the darkest and harshest veils known to man shall be set free and washed by the blood of My Son, the Lord Jesus Christ. And the veil and scales of deception shall be removed from their eyes and they shall walk in the light as I AM in the Light. Some will feel compelled by My love to re-cross your borders while others will hurry back down the Tunnel to the continent and beyond to share with others who are living under this harsh regime. They will share what they have witnessed and experienced, of another Rider who sits astride a white horse and is truly Faithful and True. With eyes that blaze like fire, dressed in a robe dipped in blood who is the King of kings and Lord of lords.

"Truly, truly I say to America and Britain, be prepared to see a level of repentance hitherto not seen on such a scale that you are about to experience, not even in the times of Edwards, Wesley, Whitefield, Finney, Roberts, Campbell[3] and all the others who have gone before as I pour out My Spirit on you for My glory."

Michael Backholer, 1 October 2010 – www.ProphecyNow.co.uk

1. Midnight, 14 May 1948, the State of Israel was proclaimed.
2. In January 2010, a 7.0-magnitude earthquake hit Haiti.
3. See *Revival Fires and Awakenings* by Mathew Backholer.

Chapter 6

Personal Responsibility

'Sow for yourselves righteousness; reap in mercy; break up your fallow ground, for it is time to seek the Lord, till He comes and rains righteousness on you' (Hosea 10:12).

The Last Minutes of the Final Hour
(Worship in Spirit and in Truth – I will Pour out My Spirit)

This is what the Sovereign Lord says to His Church,

"For generations My people have sung, 'Let all the world in every corner sing, "My God and King." ' So I ask, do you truly have an expectation in your hearts for this to happen? All over the world My children sing praises to Me and yet for many their hearts are far from Me. Too often it is only words they have been taught by others. They sing songs, the words of which have little or no true meaning in their hearts, and furthermore, were they to analyse those words they would discover in truth they don't believe some of them anyway. Do not their own children in their child-like way do the very same thing?

"So I say to My children born of My Spirit, I have called you to worship Me in Spirit and in truth, for I am in the process of pouring out My Spirit on all flesh just as I promised in My Word. So, be matured by the reading of My Word and open to receive all that I have for you. Do not resist what I am doing in these last days because I know what is best for you. You need to be filled with My Spirit, if you truly desire My will to be done on earth as it is in Heaven.

"Bad news travels fast in torrents around the earth and before you can take in what is happening and come to terms with it, another disaster strikes and things appear to go from bad to worse. And the faith of many fails them at this hour and the love of most grows cold by the day. But I say, be encouraged. I AM Sovereign and all that is written in My Word shall come to pass.

"You were warned well in advance what to expect, but remember you have the good news, don't let go of it. Hold onto those truths in your hearts, and look up, your redemption draws nigh and all over the world, men, women and children will sing out for all to hear, 'My God and King.' And remember, I shall return at an hour you least expect."

Michael Backholer, 4 Sept. 2006 – www.ProphecyNow.co.uk

Those who Play with Fire will Get Burnt!
(Sifting and Shaking)

This is what the Sovereign Lord says,

"Listen, listen I say. This is not the time to be playing with fire, you will get burnt. Some of you are already singed and yet continue to play in and around the flames. My generals, and indeed all My people know the flames may seem warm and inviting for a season, but they will dry you out and before you know it, you to will burst into flames, and be consumed and bring further shame on My house.

"There is a sifting and a shaking going on which is of Me, and this is for your own good as I prepare My Church for these last days. Yet, some of you are hell-bent and delude yourselves into thinking that you are somehow different from the rest. I tell you plainly you have become deceived by the evil one into believing that you can turn away from the flames anytime you choose. But I warn you, you are heading the same way as the others.

"Now, now, now is the time to turn and flee and call on the name of the Lord. Cry out to Me, confess and repent of your sin. Yes, while there is still time or you to will be thrown to one side, and be left to smoulder alone to bare the shame and disgrace of your actions. Reach out to Me now, before it is too late and I will lift you out of the flames. Wipe the smoke filled tears from your eyes and believe My promise:

" 'God is not a man, that He should lie, nor a son of man that He should change His mind. Does He speak and then not act? Does He promise and not fulfil?' " (Numbers 23:19), NIV.

Michael Backholer, 24 Nov. 2006 – www.ProphecyNow.co.uk

A Warning
(Those who only Love God in Measure)

This is what the Sovereign Lord says to His Church,

"Even now, says the Lord, even now, there are many in My Body who proclaim Me as Lord, yet still only want Me on their terms. Oh yes, they call out to Me from time to time, 'O Lord,' they say, 'O Lord,' as if I was the only one in the world who really mattered to them, yet in truth, behind that thin and fragile veneer that they project for all to see, they only love Me in measure. Yes that's right, they only love Me in measure and furthermore, there are those whom I have called into My service and still refuse to come. There are others who came and I anointed them to minister to My Body, yes My Body, the Body of Christ which My beloved Son is the Head of and died for – sadly they have taken My anointing and gifts to further their own plans, not mine. What of My glory I ask? Yes, what of My glory?

"What I have tolerated in the past I will not tolerate in the future. For a season you have deceived yourselves and others, thinking it was acceptable, but it is not, and I give you fair warning. Have I not been patient with you? Yes, I have, but be warned, man's heart is deceitful. Above all things, I the Lord search the heart of man and examine their minds to reward them according to their conduct, according to what their deeds deserve.

"Do not think that these rewards are only for now in this life, for they are not. So take time and examine yourselves in light of My Word, then turn and repent, before all that is truly in your heart is discovered."

Michael Backholer, 5 Feb. 2007 – www.ProphecyNow.co.uk

Jesus said, "Why do you call Me, 'Lord, Lord,' and do not do the things which I say?" (Luke 6:46). God commands us to 'be holy' (1 Peter 1:16), to 'walk uprightly' (Psalm 15:2) and we *must* have 'clean hands and a pure heart' (Psalm 24:3-6), because without holiness 'no one will see the Lord' (Hebrews 12:14). See also Isaiah chapter 58, Hosea 10:12 and Matthew 5:1-12.

End-Time Strategy – Pray for your Leadership
(Temptations will Come like Waves and Floods)

This is what the Sovereign Lord says to His Church,

"Listen, it is important that you have some measure of understanding, of the devil's end-time strategy as he directs horde after horde of evil / unclean spirits to attack and entice those in positions of authority in My Church, and so cause them to slip or fall. It is important that you plead and pray the protection of the blood of the Lord Jesus Christ over all those I have placed over you. For these will indeed be times of great testing for those without the full armour of God to protect them.

"All areas of the flesh which have not been crucified will be tried and tested to the full, time and time again. Temptations will come like waves and floods, and those who are weak and unprepared, having given little or no thought to spiritual warfare will feel the full force of the enemy as they attack every area of their souls.

"For some in the West who are comfortable and unprepared, do not smirk at these warnings as you do so at your own peril. So I say again, plead and pray daily for all in leadership because only those who are refined by the fire shall enter into the end-time blessings of My Church."

Michael Backholer, 28 Nov. 2006 – www.ProphecyNow.co.uk

The Bible tells us to 'test the spirits' (1 John 4:1), because there is much which is false; deceiving spirits and their lies which are doctrines of demons! (1 Timothy 4:1-3). '...There will be false teachers among you, who secretly bring in destructive heresies...many will follow their destructive ways...' (2 Peter 2:1-2). Wolves in sheep's clothing (Matthew 7:15). 'But evil men and impostors will grow worse...deceiving and be deceived' (2 Timothy 3:13). 'Do not be carried about with various and strange doctrines...' (Hebrews 13:9). 'Even if we, or an angel from Heaven preach any other gospel to you than what we have preached to you, let him be accursed' (Gal. 1:8). 'Supplications, prayers, intercessions...be made for all men, for kings and all who are in authority...' (1 Timothy 2:1-2).

Chapter 7

Intercessors – Spiritual Warfare (Rees Howells)

'To the intent that now the manifold wisdom of God might be made known by the Church to the principalities and powers in the Heavenly places' (Ephesians 3:10).

End-Time Preparations for the End-Time Move of the Spirit (Releasing Faith and Looking for Overcomers)

This is what the Sovereign Lord says,

"In this season of end-time preparations I am releasing faith to My Body for without faith, true faith, you will be unable to accomplish all that I have called My Church to be. Were not My disciples hidden for a time behind locked doors through fear of the enemy? But I empowered them and out they came, full of faith to turn their world upside down; so shall it be in this season.

"I shall release faith to move mountains, mountains of unbelief, mountains of sickness and disease, mountains of torment and bondage, mountains of poverty; yes, yes, even faith for creative miracles, faith to overcome all the works of the enemy.

"I am looking for vessels who will become overcomers, those who believe Me, not just for the possible, but for the impossible. Those who will go where I send them, even though they know not where they are going or where they may lay their head, or if they shall return; faith to speak to leaders, governments and kings. This will call for no ordinary faith, but extraordinary, a supernatural faith which is only found in Me.

"Are YOU willing to be a part of this end-time move of My Spirit? Are YOU willing to forsake all for the gospel of your Lord and Saviour?"

Michael Backholer, 15 March 2007 – www.ProphecyNow.co.uk

GO ye (Mark 16:15), GIVE ye (Luke 9:13) and PRAY ye (Matthew 9:38). SERVE Him, OBEY Him and ABIDE in Him.

Intercessors Called to Warfare, Prepare the Way for the Evangelists and Revivalists – (Rees Howells)

This is what the Sovereign Lord says,

"I am calling forth men and women from the nations of the earth who are willing to forsake all, follow Me, crucify their flesh and die to self daily; those who will not count or consider the cost or look back. Those who are willing to make up the hedge and stand in the gap before Me on behalf of the land as did My servant and My friend Rees Howells, who knew the secret place of abiding in Me. He was willing for My Spirit to work through him to intercede and bind the strong man, pull down strongholds, and dislodge principalities and powers of darkness and all spiritual forces of evil.

"I call the ones who have been through the fire and walked the wilderness path, for I have prepared them for such a time as this. These are the ones that have been despised and looked down upon, but now in this hour I shall raise them up as part of My battle plan, they know My voice and are obedient to My Word. They will not compromise with man or the world, for they are wholly Mine and shall go forth, led of My Spirit to prepare the way for the evangelists and revivalists, some of whom are one and the same, and I shall use them for My glory and My glory alone.

"These are the anointed ones; 'Do not touch My anointed ones; do My prophets no harm,' 'For who can lay a hand on the Lord's anointed and be guiltless?' "

Michael Backholer, 2 January 2007 – www.ProphecyNow.co.uk

The Every Creature Commission
(Rees Howells, Intercession and Warfare)

This is what the Sovereign Lord says,

"In the days of Isaiah and Hezekiah, I gave a sign of My promise to them that the shadow cast by the sun would retreat the ten steps it had gone down on the stairway of Ahaz [2 Kings

20:8-11 and Isaiah 38:7-8]. Nothing has changed; My promises are as current coin from one generation to any other. The Pharisees and experts in the law in their generation rejected My purpose for their lives by refusing to be baptised by John the Baptist. In the parable of the persistent widow, Jesus taught that I will bring about justice for My chosen ones who cry out to Me day and night. I also inquired whether I would find faith on the earth. [A rhetorical question].

"So now we come to these end-time generations and the faith and unity required to bring about My purposes on earth as in Heaven. This is not the time to be thinking about having a good time, but there are good times to be had. This is not the time to be thinking about the cost, but there is a price to be paid, and this is definitely not the time to be self-centred, but centred on My Son. For I am sorely troubled by the fact that many in the Church today, still have little or no understanding of the true nature and purpose of its calling or My purpose for it. My intent is that now, through the Church, My manifold wisdom should be made known to the rulers and authorities in the Heavenly realms, according to My eternal purpose which was accomplished in Christ Jesus [see Ephesians 3:10-11]. Not a legacy of inward fighting and petty squabbles where the uncrucified flesh is more important than the Every Creature Commission. [Matthew 28:18-20 and Mark 16:15].

"So, I bring to your attention a few who have gone before, who laid down their lives for the gospel, and cried out to Me day and night for justice, and to prepare the way for others to follow. So, it is in these last days I called for a man to stand in the gap on behalf of others and chose one from beneath the Black Mountains of Wales (in the UK), and in the fullness of time he [Rees Howells] was sown as a seed in the cleft of a rock overlooking Swansea Bay. Then I called forth other seeds who were chosen for their faith and they were grafted in, and they were transformed by the Holy Spirit, as each in turn surrendered their will for Mine; for a season of combined faith for spiritual warfare on the earth, and in the Heavenly realms on a scale not witnessed before, as each did their part, led by My Spirit. They too were given a sign as a promise that the Every Creature Commission would be fulfilled and the finances required released.

"Knowing that I found faith on the earth for the gospel to reach all of mankind, the devil spurred on by his hatred of Me and My creation unleashed the powers of darkness and did everything he could to influence the outcome, bringing about catastrophic consequences throughout the earth. But at every turn it was met with a wall of faith that restrained them [principalities and powers] until finally bound, driven back, & victory was assured in keeping with the Word of God and My promises. Except a corn of wheat fall into the ground and die, it abideth alone; but if it die, it bringeth forth much fruit. Having died to self, they were raised up in Christ, to live to see the fruit of their warfare and the ongoing fruit of their intercessions continue to this day and will continue to bear fruit as I pour out My Spirit on all people.

"The seeds of the first fruits are sown, the authentic cleft in the rock has been relocated and the bridge that led to it has been torn down [places associated with Rees Howells]. But the true and genuine legacy is still being released throughout the earth as promised with a new generation of disciples who have surrendered all to the Holy Spirit and will be raised up in Christ to complete Jesus' last command, in the power of the Spirit."

Michael Backholer, 3 Nov. 2010 – www.ProphecyNow.co.uk

There are many Christians who love to hear what God is doing; missionary stories, testimonies of deliverances, healings and miracles – they love to be entertained by the workings of God in and through people's lives. 'Their mouth shows much love, but their hearts pursue their own gain' wrote Ezekiel. 'Indeed you are to them as a very lovely song of one who has a pleasant voice.' These stories excite their emotions, but when you challenge them to a greater commitment or full surrender to God (Romans 12:1, Galatians 2:20 and 2 Corinthians 5:15), 'they hear your words, but they do not do them' (Ezekiel 33:31-33). They are not prepared to take up their cross, deny themselves, forsake sin, follow the Master or abide in the Vine!

A "gospel" message of easy-believism – free grace and God's love, without repentance, obligations and responsibilities (to forsake sin and the world; to embrace Jesus Christ and the cross, to live unreservedly and wholeheartedly for Him) is a great disservice for all concerned. We must be 'born again' (John 3:3, 7) and pass from 'death to life' (1 John 3:14).

My Will, My Power by My Spirit in the Last Days
(One in the Spirit – The Every Creature Commission)

This is what the Sovereign Lord says,

"To those who claim in My name to be My Church in the nations of the world, from the centre to the outer most parts of the four winds – If you will not give Me your bodies as your spiritual act of worship, then give Me your ear to hear what I have to say to each and every one of you. Who truly lives in your body? Who are you truly led by? Is your body truly a temple of the Holy Spirit?

"Many, not just a few, claim they are filled with My Spirit yet do not abide (remain) in the Vine. Nor have they embraced the cross, truly repented or crucified their old self; for those who truly belong to Jesus have crucified the sinful nature. This is why you are controlled by your passions and desires, and your minds are set on earthy things instead of your hearts being set on things above – My Kingdom and My will. Many are mechanical, even automatic as you operate without conscious thought of the Holy Spirit, in your own strength and your own will. My good, pleasing and perfect will is that you be conformed into the image of Jesus, obey My Word and walk as He did. How can you claim to be in the light, as He is in the light, yet continue to walk in the shadow of darkness? Are you not foolish? Bewitched? Have you not added your own rules and regulations that oppress and crush the life of the Spirit out of the people in the name of your group or denomination?

"Give heed to what you believe and what I say, for in the day and the hour of My return you could find yourself assigned a place with the hypocrites with the weeping and gnashing of teeth. Listen I say, listen, to what for many remains a mystery, an enigma. I have a remnant in the Body of Christ, in the Church, who abide day and night and are called My friends. They are a storehouse of polished cogs that the Holy Spirit indwells at the very centre and heart of their beings. They shine like the noonday sun, like lamps, wise ones with oil to spare. They have been called, set apart, and come from all walks and diverse backgrounds, in all shapes and sizes. Yet they coexist and synchronise as one in time and Spirit, a living, vibrant remnant who will mesh together for My glory. Intercessors, apostles, prophets and evangelists who have been called, chosen, appointed, anointed, and will hear a voice saying, 'This is the way walk in it.'

"Go into all the world and complete the Every Creature Commission in keeping with My Word, and the intercessions of My Holy Spirit, working through the surrendered bodies of those warriors in Wales, who have now fallen to the ground as a seed of corn; and others who chose to walk as Nash and Finney did. All different, but all made one, different gifts, but one Spirit, different in service, but one Lord. Different ways of working but one God, like cogs all working in harmony, all doing their part in the unity of the Spirit with equal concern for each other; as one is moved by the Spirit to do its part, so in turn, all are moved in different directions to do their part. One in spirit, one in purpose, one in love, all in the power of the Spirit in My will."

Michael Backholer, Easter Weekend, (April 2012) – www.ProphecyNow.co.uk

The Work and Legacy of the Holy Spirit
(An Ongoing Living Legacy from Generation to Generation)

This is what the Sovereign Lord says,

"Let it be known throughout the lands, My Kingdom will come and My will shall be done. Old wells, old pals and their networks cannot prise or profit from the work of the Holy Spirit.

"The high Heavens belong to the Lord, but He gave the earth to man. Man may purchase a plot of land, on which the Holy Spirit has dug a well, in and through the sweat, blood and tears of others who have laid down their lives, as a seed of corn in previous generations. But the living water in the well always remains with the Lord; until such times that the new owner pays the full price in God's currency of unconditional surrender of one's body, mind and will.

"In these days of instant tea, coffee, mash-potato and automatic washing machines, there is no instant or automatic right, or way to receive the Holy Spirit's anointing or to walk in His power. As Simon of Samaria, a captive of sin, learnt to his cost. He could not purchase the Holy Spirit or His anointing and had no part, or share in God's work [Acts 8:5-24].

"The Holy Spirit's spiritual gifts are indeed gifts, given for the common good. But His fruit, the fruit of His character and His power and anointing comes at a cost. The Holy Spirit as a Person, entered the life of Jesus, as gentle as a dove at His baptism, and it was the Holy Spirit who led Jesus from the Jordan River into the wilderness. Jesus having overcome all of the temptations of the devil, returned to Galilee in the power of the Holy Spirit!

"It was the acts of the Holy Spirit working in and through the bodies and minds of Jesus' disciples that turned their world upside down. There is resurrection power available to all who are called and chosen, after the crucifixion of their flesh and self-will. That is the price to be paid.

"The legacy and the inheritance of Rees and Samuel Rees Howells and their team, is not to be found on the former site of the Bible College of Wales, but in the abiding faith of the cross, the blood, and in the Holy Spirit as a Person, and in His will. It is He who will guide you into all truth and it He who brings true conviction to the world of guilt, regarding sin. Without His true conviction, there can be no true repentance, forgiveness or rebirth.

"Many in this generation are running here, there and everywhere after an anointing or a double-portion of another's spirit. Rees Howells, his son Samuel, and the staff members of the former Bible College of Wales learned that without the Holy Spirit, they could do nothing when they came to face the enemy in spiritual warfare.

"The true and everlasting legacy was not theirs to give to others, or for others to take, but for those like them in every generation, who abide in the Vine, as a branch. It is the Holy Spirit and the intercessions He made through them that counts. The flesh counts for nothing.

"It is the work of the Holy Spirit that endures and is everlasting. He bears all, and suffers in and through those bodies where He resides and abides, in the Father's perfect will – just as Jesus did while on the earth, and continues to do so while sat at God's right hand, interceding for the saints.

"Rees Howells and his team of intercessors offered their bodies as living sacrifices, holy and pleasing to God, as their spiritual act of worship. They no longer conformed to the pattern of the world by the transforming and renewing of their minds. By so doing, they were able to test and approve what My good, pleasing and perfect will was, by allowing the Holy Spirit to make them one in spirit and in truth. He interceded through them and the world was turned upside down once again in their generation. Without the Person of the Holy Spirit living in their fully surrendered bodies, there would never have been any intercession, or legacy.

"The Holy Spirit is the only Person living on the earth today who was present at the crucifixion and the resurrection. He and He alone is the only true Intercessor, legacy and birthright of the Body of Christ. He is the Spirit of Truth, just as Jesus is the Way, the Truth and the Life. When you embrace and abide with the Holy Spirit, you embrace and abide with the Father and the Son also. It is foolishness to believe that the Body of Christ can fulfil the Great Commission without the Holy Spirit having full possession of your bodies as His temples."

Michael Backholer, 5 June 2012 – www.ProphecyNow.co.uk

If you desire to have a deeper and more intimate relationship with the Father and the Son through the Holy Spirit, or you wish to know what the Holy Spirit can achieve through an individual, or a company of believers made one in spirit and in truth in love, then read *Samuel Rees Howells: A Life of Intercession* by Richard Maton, and *Holy Spirit Power* by Paul Backholer.

- Jesus spoke of the promise of the Father, the Holy Spirit (Luke 24:49, John 14:16-17, John 16:7-15 and Acts 1:8).
- God will give the Holy Spirit to those who obey Him – not the disobedient (Acts 5:32).
- Your Heavenly Father will give the Holy Spirit to those who ask – have you? (Luke 11:13).
- The Holy Spirit will not come and fill dirty vessels (Isaiah 52:11b). Be holy because God is holy (1 Peter 1:16).
- Grieve not the Holy Spirit (Ephesians 4:30-31).
- Do not resist the Holy Spirit (Acts 7:51 and Proverbs 29:1).
- Do not quench the Holy Spirit (1 Thessalonians 5:19-20).
- Be filled with the Holy Spirit – are you? (Ephesians 5:18).

A Graceful Chain of Intercessors
(The Great Commission – End-time Outpouring)

This is what the Sovereign Lord says,

"It is written that Jesus was anointed with a fragrant perfume by a woman whilst staying in a house in Bethany. It is also written that wherever the gospel is preached in the world, what she did will also be told in memory of her. So, I say unto you this day, write this down as something to be remembered and made known to others:

"I am forming a chain of grace through faith, a chain of intercessors all linked together as one by My Spirit. Now in the fullness of My time, it will encompass the whole earth in Spirit and in truth. They are all a part of a remnant that I have hidden in the cleft of My rock, the Rock of Ages. They seek not the things of this world and care not for fame or fortune. Their only desire is to be obedient to the Holy Spirit and abide with Him so He can do His work of intercession in and through them.

"These are the ones that I have set apart, called, appointed and anointed to bear fruit that will last. They have embraced the cross of crucifixion and placed everything on the altar of sacrifice. These are the ones that truly love Me, not in measure but with all their heart, soul, strength and mind, for they are truly Mine.

"Again I say unto you, write this down as something to remember and make it known to others. Rees and Samuel Rees Howells and their team of co-workers at the former Bible College of Wales (UK), gave everything they had for the glory of God to help bring the gospel to every creature (The Great Commission Matthew 28:18-20 and Mark 16:15). Let it be known, write it down in their memory that it is the Holy Spirit working in and through this new chain of intercessors that Rees and Samuel Rees Howells and their team believed for, who will bind the strong man and pull down his strongholds which are many, in preparation for the completion of the end-time outpouring of the Holy Spirit from on high."

Michael Backholer, 7 June 2012 – www.ProphecyNow.co.uk

Links with the Holy Spirit
(Linked with the Holy Spirit or Chained by the Devil?)

This is what the Sovereign Lord says,

"I have spoken to you and revealed to you about My chain of grace, of intercessors who are all linked together as one in spirit and in truth, by the Holy Spirit encompassing the earth. I have made known to you through the Word, the great chain that the angel will use to bind the dragon for a thousand years.

"But I am grieved that many of My people are bound and chained due to the lack of knowledge of the Holy Spirit. They boast of their social links, and are pleased, even proud of their links on their web pages. For many the internet has become a net that pulls them further and further from My will and My Holy Spirit. Tell Me this day are you linked with the Holy Spirit or are you chained by the devil?

"Is your name written on a page in the Book of Life? You call Me, 'Lord, Lord,' but am I truly Lord and Saviour of your lives? Many, far too many are still infants in Christ. Men are still boasting of their links, little has changed since the days of Paul and Apollos.

"There is only one foundation to build on, Jesus Christ. One plan, plan A, My will done, in My way, in My time. You are outside My conception of time and for many outside of My will also. There are large gatherings of My people, and large ministries who are building on gold, silver and costly stones that will not withstand the test of the fire of the Holy Spirit.

"I tell you the truth, Apollos an educated man with a thorough knowledge of the Scriptures spoke with great fervour. But, Aquila and Priscilla taught him the way of God more accurately for they were linked in Spirit and in truth to the Holy Spirit, and desired to be chained to His will. These tent makers like Paul had learned to live and abide with the Holy Spirit daily, unlike so many today who claim they will enter Heaven as their birthright, and in their next breath blaspheme the Holy Spirit and speak against Him, for which there is no forgiveness. This is an eternal sin in this age and in the age to come; think long and hard about this, meditate on it day and night, then ask yourself has the Holy Spirit truly entered into your life, into your body as

His temple? Do you truly eat together? It is the ones who overcome that have a right to Heaven. He who has ears, hear what the Spirit of the Lord says to the churches, it will be the overcomers who have the right to eat from the tree of life in the Paradise of God.

"Now ask yourselves, why are so many of your fellowships dead or dying? Why are so many of your buildings empty? Why does revival tarry? Are you looking to Me? Truly I ask you, truly answer Me, who are you looking to? Who are you waiting for? For I AM looking to you, waiting for you to do your part in Spirit and in truth, I AM truly grieved for the Kingdom of Heaven's net is nearing fullness and will be pulled up."

Michael Backholer, 8 June 2012 – www.ProphecyNow.co.uk

Some Christians who have actively sought for and prayed for revival will reject it when God sends it; because the effects and results were different than what they had anticipated. Rejecting revival is rejecting the Holy Spirit – rejecting God Himself! The Pharisees and Sadducees missed the day of visitation when the Messiah (Jesus Christ) came, yet they had the Scriptures which foretold His life (John 5:39-40), and they got upset with those who embraced Him! (Luke 19:42-44). God can also bless one church, yet bypass another in the same town! We all need to be careful that we do not miss the day of visitation (1 Peter 2:12b), when the showers of blessing fall (Ezekiel 34:26), the former and the latter rain (Joel 2:23). See *Revival Answers, True and False Revivals* by Mathew Backholer. Let us not be too hesitant to move into the River of God. Some at first may appear paralysed, unable to roll up their trouser legs and paddle, let alone wade, but like in Ezekiel's day, the river flows from the temple and only in steps may we walk into the river. Up to our ankles, then our knees, and up to our waist until we are immersed in the River of God which is life giving, refreshing, reviving and brings healing to the nations (Ezekiel 47 and Revelation 22:1-5). However, let us not frolic in the River of God and neglect our duty, "Go into all the world, and preach the gospel to every creature," commanded Jesus Christ (Mark 16:15). See also Matthew 28:18-20, Luke 24:47-49, John 20:21-23 and Acts 1:8. The Great Commission is *our* commission! What have we done about it?

Chapter 8

Harvesters and the Coming Harvest

Jesus said, "...Behold, I say to you, lift up your eyes and look at the fields, for they are already white for harvest! And he who reaps receives wages and gathers fruit for eternal life that both he who sows and he who reaps may rejoice" (John 4:35b-36).

Ask, Seek and Knock and Fully Surrender Yourselves (Harvesters Needed!)

This is what the Sovereign Lord says to His Church,

"To the many in the Church who feel discouraged, disheartened, defeated and powerless, I have this to say, 'My power is made perfect in weakness, for My Kingdom is not a matter of words but of power, the power of My Holy Spirit which is available to all who ask.' How much more will I give My Holy Spirit to those who ask, this is My promise to all who ask, seek and knock sincerely. Furthermore, My anointing is available to all who will not count the cost, and surrender their bodies to My Holy Spirit who will make it His temple, and cleanse and restore it, and make it holy; for without holiness no one will see the Lord. This is a sacrifice, holy and pleasing to Me, your spiritual act of worship, and do not conform any longer to the pattern of this world, but be transformed by the renewing of your minds. Then you will be able to test and approve what My will is – My good, pleasing and perfect will.

"I am looking for men and women from every nation who will surrender their lives fully to My will and become My disciples. They must live in obedience to My Word, and My Holy Spirit, so We can work in and through them to help bring in the greatest harvest ever known, in preparation for that great and glorious day when every knee shall bow and tongue confess, 'Jesus Christ is Lord.' "

Michael Backholer, 6 Sept. 2006 – www.ProphecyNow.co.uk

A Youth Army is Arising – Harvesters are Making Ready
(Strong and keen to Share the Good News)

This is what the Sovereign Lord says,

"I hear the footsteps of a generation of young people born for such a time as this, their feet are stamping, stamping, stamping, ready for the gallop. They are strong and keen to share the good news of the Kingdom of their God. They are pulling at the reins, longing for My reign, longing to go forth into the darkness of the world, to bring the light of My salvation to all who will listen. They are radical, forceful and willing to advance in every direction.

"This is the generation the prophets have spoken of and the intercessors have prayed for. Their families, friends and leaders will not recognise them at first and be alarmed, for I shall empower them from on high. Homes, brothers, sisters, mothers, fathers or fields will not hold them back. These will be the end-time disciples who consider it an honour to share in persecutions and suffer for the sake of the gospel.

"A cry will go up, 'Who will provide for so many?' Oh selfish ones and comfortable ones, who fed the multitudes? Who sent the twelve and the seventy-two out with nothing for their journey? Oh you of little faith, did they not all return with joy and even the demons submitted to them in My name, but they rejoiced that their names were written in Heaven. The harvest is plentiful and the harvesters are making ready."

Michael Backholer, 9 Feb. 2007 – www.ProphecyNow.co.uk

- '...It is good to be zealous in a good thing...' (Gal. 4:18).
- 'Declare His glory among the nations, His wonders among all peoples' (Psalm 96:3).
- 'Arise, O God, judge the earth; for You shall inherit all nations' (Psalm 82:8).
- 'I will go in the strength of the Lord God; I will make mention of Your righteousness, of Yours only' (Psalm 71:16).
- 'That men may know that You, whose name alone is the Lord, are the Most High over all the earth' (Psalm 83:18).

The Grey Haired Soldiers of the Cross
(Most Useful – Full of Faith and Wisdom)

This is what the Sovereign Lord says,

"Many have spoken about the youth army I am raising up, but there is another army, long forgotten, which I have not overlooked and will use much to the surprise of many. I speak of the grey haired soldiers of the cross, who are full of faith and wisdom. They may not be youthful, but they are most useful and I shall use them for My purposes, for they shall enter doors that I shall open which others would tremble at.

"They have a lifetime of experience that they can call upon, and have prayed and believed for many of the youth that I shall also use for My purposes. Therefore, it is expedient that I should use them at this time, for they know how to reach the Throne Room of Heaven and call down power and protection for those who are zealous and youthful."

"Do not forget that they too were once young in body, but through long and arduous campaigns kept the home-fires burning, ready for the day when I would again blow on the embers and cause flames to leap into action for all to see. Flames that shall leap from one generation to another, from one place to another; from hamlets to villages, from villages to towns, from towns to cities and from cities to the nations."

Michael Backholer, 12 May 2007 – www.ProphecyNow.co.uk

The End-Time Harvest – Combine with the Holy Spirit
(Plead for the Nations – Anointed to Minister)

This is what the Sovereign Lord says,

"From the days of John the Baptist until now, the Kingdom of Heaven has been forcefully advancing and forceful men lay hold of it (Matthew 11:12). With the passing of the seasons, those who were willing have prayed and ploughed through the rough places of their hearts, and welcomed, and worked with the Holy Spirit's harrow, enabling them to sow the seeds of righteousness, and reap the fruit of unfailing love. For now is the time to seek the Lord of the harvest until He comes and showers down righteousness. The heart of man is deceitful, and every heart shall be searched, and every mind examined to be rewarded as their deeds deserve.

"There are many in the house of God wearing a Sunday smile on their faces, but their hearts are far from Me. Have I not decreed that My house should be a house of prayer for all nations, and that My people should petition the Lord of the harvest to send out harvesters into the harvest field? Have I not said, 'If,' yes, 'if' My people, not when, but if My people will humble themselves, and pray and seek My face, and turn away; yes I say, again and again, turn away from your wicked ways, then shall I hear, and forgive their sin, yes, their sin, and come and heal their land.

"Many in this hour cry out to Me for new cars or to win the lottery, but few cry out for souls to be saved, and fail to understand their true state, of being morally and spiritually bankrupt. Let those who have ears, hear, and understand what the Spirit of God is saying to the Church. You have placed your faith in human ability and the finances that you are able to raise and have bankrupted the Church of true faith and real power. But I am raising up and releasing men and women of faith who shall walk in the power of My Spirit. This is the season of the combine, a time to combine as one with the Holy Spirit to bring in the most stupendous, and by far the greatest portion of the end-time harvest ever witnessed, with signs and wonders confirming the preaching of My Word.

"All of mankind and every nation will be offered life and forgiveness, and at this time, it is essential that My people plead for the nations and release a heartfelt cry from deep within, where I have placed My deposit of life that resides within them. It is a reflection of My love and power, as a positive force and witness that will release the angelic forces to disarm, overpower and dislodge the spiritual powers and forces of darkness in the Heavenly realms. The Kingdom of God is not a matter of talk, but of power."

Michael Backholer, 14 Dec. 2010 – www.ProphecyNow.co.uk

Chapter 9

The Holy Spirit

The apostle Paul wrote: 'If the ministry of death, written and engraved on stones was glorious, so that the children of Israel could not look steadily at the face of Moses because of the glory of his countenance, which glory was passing away, how will the ministry of the Spirit not be more glorious?' (2 Corinthians 3:7-8).

The Last Days – This Age Draws to a Close (Looking for Vessels to be Filled with My Spirit)

This is what the Sovereign Lord says,

"Even now, even now at this late hour as this age draws to a close, My Spirit looks throughout the earth for men and women who I can use for My glory in these last days. I am looking for more than a temple for My Spirit to live in, I am looking for vessels that I can fill and reveal My glory through – those who are willing to forsake all others, and lay down their lives daily, for My glory, and Mine alone.

"No longer will I suffer the lukewarm or the double-minded. I have had My fill of the double-minded in these last generations; mouths that are full of empty promises, cheap words that bring forth shallow and often little commitment. The double-minded are unstable in all they do. I am looking for oaks whose roots go deep into the Rock of their salvation; are you such a one?

"Consider carefully how you answer, for words come cheap; first, wash your hands you sinners and purify your hearts you double-minded. For I loathe the double-minded who say one thing and then turn away to do something different. Away from Me, Pharisee, hypocrite, I am looking, searching, calling for disciples; not church-goers with the nickname Christian. If this offends you, then, you are not one of those that I seek."

Michael Backholer, 18 Nov. 2007 – www.ProphecyNow.co.uk

Will you Reject God
(Will YOU Dictate to the Holy Spirit?)

This is what the Sovereign Lord says,

"Have you not read, 'take captive every thought to make it obedient to Christ,' and, 'this is love that we walk in obedience to His commands?' Obedience to the Lord's commands is obedience that comes from faith and this obedience leads to righteousness. Are you aware that I have access to your innermost thoughts that are hidden from others in the deep recesses of your mind? Nothing is hidden from Me.

"I hear the murmurings of a people just like the ones in the wilderness. I also hear the arrogant and presumptuous boasts of others who believe they know better than their Maker. I have heard it said behind closed doors and openly:

'We do not want *that* here.'

'We do not want *that* kind of thing in *our* church.'

'This sort of *thing* offends many and they might leave.'

'Lets not rock the boat, we are okay as we are; we do not want a split.'

'Do not mention sin or repentance, it only puts people off.'

'Anyway, realistically speaking, you cannot expect people in this day and age to be holy.'

"You may not expect it, but I AM, and, I do; without holiness no one will see the Lord. Furthermore, I am the Head of the Church, and My supernatural power and Presence, which you mockingly refer to as 'this and that,' is the power of My Holy Spirit. The very power that can transform lives and anyone who speaks against My Holy Spirit will not be forgiven.

"When you reject the Holy Spirit, you also reject the Father and the Son, for We are One. Jesus did not come to the earth to bring peace, but a sword, and the cross is, and always will be, an offence to many. If the Holy Spirit is not made welcome, or is grieved in your presence, then He will depart from among you, and all you will be left with is your flesh. So consider carefully, what truly is of the flesh, and that which is of My Spirit.

"In Elijah's day, I reserved seven thousand in Israel for My glory and today I have thousands more in the world, a remnant who will do My will, for My glory without fear of man. They will go in the power of the Spirit to the highways and byways and into the marketplaces of the world, and My Spirit will bring conviction of guilt in regards to sin, righteousness and judgment. "When the people see a demonstration of My power and feel the heat that emanates from the fire of conviction poured out from on high (as in Elijah's day, on Mount Carmel), the people will fall to the ground and declare, 'The Lord He is God!' But some will say, 'This is the flesh. God would not do this.' But I have, I AM, and I will continue to do so. Remember, without My Spirit all you have is the flesh, let those who have ears hear."

Michael Backholer, 26 July 2010 – www.ProphecyNow.co.uk

Jesus said, "You shall receive power when the Holy Spirit has come upon you and you shall be witnesses to Me..." (Acts 1:8).

The Holy Spirit or Ichabod
(To Embrace or Reject the Spirit of God)

This is what the Sovereign Lord says,

"It is written: 'You stiff-necked people with uncircumcised hearts and ears! You are just like your fathers; you always resist the Holy Spirit!' (Acts 7:51). Yes indeed, says the Lord, there is nothing new under the sun. Many of My people have quaint little sayings [devoid of personal experiences], none of which have little or nothing to do with My plans or purposes. For example, "You may have the Holy Spirit, but does He have you?" This may impress some, but more to the point, and shout it from your pulpits, if the truth be made known, few indeed I say, yes few indeed, truly know the Holy Spirit as a Person, and even fewer are led by Him.

"It has become fashionable once again, to quote, 'You shall know the truth and the truth will set you free.' The truth is this: there are many places where people meet in My name, but My Holy Spirit is not welcome there and yet, We are One. They claim to be My disciples and claim I am in their midst. 'Ichabod' I say, 'Ichabod!' [1 Samuel 4:20-22]. My glory departed long ago with My Spirit and with His power. You are to be pitied above all others for you are self-deceived and self-deluded.

You claim to be sons of a supernatural God and at the very same time divorce yourselves from all that is supernatural. Those who are ashamed of Me take note, for I shall be ashamed of you, so repent and turn away from your wicked ways.

"Wake up I say, wake up! You teach your children of My supernatural dealings with mankind, as recorded in the Scriptures, and then deny them by your actions in your generation. And to those who are self elected and believe they are called to test and approve My every move, and whom I choose to move through, I say beware. Who made you judge and jury, for you are about to forfeit the grace that could be yours. Ask yourself, who helped you utter these things? And whose spirit spoke from your mouth?

"And what of your Seminaries and Bible Colleges, am I welcome there? They claim to teach the Way, the Truth and the Life, but many still avoid or deny My Holy Spirit His rightful place, yet He is the Spirit of Truth. He is the very One that will guide you into all truth. He is the One that brings glory to Me, and He is the One that takes from what is Mine and makes it known to you.

"Be prepared I say, be prepared, for I am releasing the ones who are truly Mine, and truly one with My Spirit. Those who abide in Me, friends who know My business and have laid down their lives for Me. When you hear of them or see them, rejoice and be glad.

"Take note I say, take note, He will not enter where He is not welcome, and if He is not welcomed into My house it ceases to be My house, no matter what you say or do. Take note I say, take note, if you refuse to embrace Him, there are others in prisons and other places of darkness that will, while you remain bound and imprisoned. What will you say? What excuses will you make? How will you explain to those around you that your God is doing the miraculous in the prisons, in the marketplace, in schools and colleges – all over the place, but not where you meet? What will you say to them? More to the point, what will you say to Me? Repent I say, repent, while there is still time."

Michael Backholer, 4 January 2011 – www.ProphecyNow.co.uk

CARLY *CHosen* *peoples* *of faith*

Chapter 10

Lakeland Revival (2008) and its lessons *unconditional love*

Thus says the Lord, "Rain down, you Heavens, from above, and let the skies pour down righteousness; let the earth open, let them bring forth salvation, and let righteousness spring up together. I the Lord have created it" (Isaiah 45:8).

✳ The Sign of the Rainbow ✳
(Look for My Promise in the Sky)

This is what the Sovereign Lord says,

"The tide has turned, the wind of change has come and the spiritual fog has lifted over the Gog and Magog Hills. Lighter, brighter nights and days are coming all over the United Kingdom of Great Britain. The pockets of light and small fires, and some of the more traditional ones are bringing forth new light and warmth that will rekindle that which was hoped for in every community.

"Look for My promise in the sky over this land for it shall surely come. Look for My rainbow, a sign of My everlasting covenant with My people in this nation. I have called you to be salt and light in the land, and your faith shall be rewarded again. So I say again, look for My rainbow; this will be no ordinary everyday rainbow. This rainbow will cause many to stop and ask, what is its meaning?

"You remember the flowers from one end of the nation to the other, laid out for all to see as a witness of a nation's grief.[1] So My rainbow will blaze high in the sky for all to see, in all its brightness and majesty, as a sign to My people that all that was foretold for this once great nation is coming soon, very soon."

Michael Backholer, 5 January 2008 – www.ProphecyNow.co.uk

1. After the death of Diana, Princess of Wales in a car crash in Paris, France, on 31 August 1997.

Igniting My Church
(Restoring My Church with Power)

This is what the Sovereign Lord says,

"Listen to Me, listen, the very thing that is lacking in My Church and the very thing that will transform and restore it, is the very same thing that has brought the most controversy to it – why?" [Think about it].

"I am restoring My Church with power, authority and a holy boldness, which of course takes time. But I am the Alpha and the Omega, who is, and who was, and who is to come; the Almighty.

"I am re-birthing that which was in the beginning and is to come, that which will restore My Church and set it on fire; set it apart from all others and the world will sit up, stand up and take notice. This is the very thing that did, and will again distinguish the true disciple from the false – those who say they believe in Me, yet fear and deny My power in these last days. This is indeed a long and difficult birth, a time of travail, a painful time, but now the birthing has started, no-one can stop it. [Think about it, a worldwide birth, not a single portal].

"This kind of birth is always messy and fraught with difficulties; that is why I have chosen midwives to work through. Yes, I have chosen them and I would say to you, do not touch My anointed ones, do My prophets no harm.

"Why do so many search for a speck of sawdust in another's eye, yet pay no attention to the plank in their own eye? The earth will be filled with the knowledge of the glory of the Lord as the waters cover the sea – before the coming of the great and dreadful Day of the Lord."

Michael Backholer, 29 July 2008 – www.ProphecyNow.co.uk

Thus says the Lord, "And it shall come to pass afterward that I will pour out My Spirit on all flesh; your sons and your daughters shall prophesy, your old men shall dream dreams, your young men shall see visions; and also on My menservants and My maidservants I will pour out My Spirit in those days" (Joel 2:28-29).

- 64 -

A Measured Response – Todd Bentley
(Compassion and Mercy)

This is what the Sovereign Lord says,

"In the light of My Word consider carefully the measure with which you have judged one of your brothers in Christ – Todd Bentley. With that same measure you also will be measured, so consider carefully your own position in Christ.

"Some of you will be surprised to learn that it is My will and intention to restore[2] and use this man again for My glory. Therefore I say again, consider carefully your own position in Christ before you dare to cast another stone, verbal or otherwise in his direction. Yes, there are lessons for the whole Body of Christ to be learned from Lakeland and his [Todd Bentley's] life, but be warned, he is not the only student in My school of faith.

"Where are those who were quick to align themselves with him and the move of My Spirit? Where are they now? They were quick to slip away into the shadows, unlike David's mighty men who fought at his side, and what of all the others who were just as keen to be seen with him, where are they now? How quickly so many have been to distance themselves from My servant in his hour of need. Did you ever stop to consider the fact that I AM Sovereign and knew from the beginning what would come to pass, and the lessons to be learnt from it?

"While you were all watching Todd, I was watching you, and I am just as disappointed with some of you, as you have been with him. So I ask you, if I am to have compassion and mercy on you, who have been very careful to keep your own sin hidden from others, but not from Me – for all have sinned and fall short of My glory – should you not also have compassion on him whose sin had been aired for all to see?

"So I say to you this Good Friday, that the good news of the gospel is that the blood of the Lord Jesus Christ was shed for all mankind, and for all their sin, not just the few. Furthermore, it was I who have caused others to come alongside Todd to minister to his needs, and so, I would remind you, that it is more blessed to give than to receive, but now it is Todd's time to receive.

"Be warned that in this hour the enemy will overcome all who have not allowed their sinful nature to be crucified; but those who do, and set their minds on what My Spirit desires, will become overcomers, My true Church. The Body of Christ has an obligation, not to the sinful nature, but to live by My Spirit, for if you are led by My Spirit, you truly are sons of God.

"As I continue to pour out My Spirit on all flesh, so the enemy will continue to prowl around like a lion seeking to destroy My work on the earth. So I say to you, do not be deceived, you will reap what you sow, and if you sow to please your sinful nature you will be destroyed by it; so do not only read My Word, but do what it says."

Michael Backholer, Friday 10 April 2009, (Good Friday) – www.ProphecyNow.co.uk

2. Scripture declares that King David was a man after God's own heart (1 Samuel 13:14, 1 Samuel 16:7, 1 Kings 15:3, 5 and Acts 13:22), yet in a moment of weakness he found another woman (Bathsheba) which led to the end of a marriage and the life of her husband. King David married Bathsheba (2 Samuel chapters 11-12), but King David's sin displeased the Lord (2 Samuel 11:27). King David was repentant and God forgave him (2 Samuel 12:13-14 and Psalm 51), but these sins did not overshadow his passion for God, as God sees the heart which was loyal to Him (1 Kings 15:3-5, 11). David's life became synonymous with all that was good and it was to him that all the other kings of Judah (his descendants) were compared, whether good or bad (1 Kings 15:11, 2 Kings 14:3, 2 Kings 16:2, 2 Kings 18:3 and 2 Kings 22:2 etc.).

Revivals are fronted by leaders who are not perfect, some are vulnerable and may have weak areas as sanctification is an ongoing work. Others may have a greater anointing than the character of Christ formed in them. James aptly pointed out: 'We all stumble in many things' (James 3:2) and only he 'who is without sin' can cast the first stone (John 8:7), yet 'all have sinned' (Romans 6:23). 'Mercy triumphs over judgment' (James 2:13) and 'whatever you want men to do to you, do also to them' (Matt. 7:12). Jesus warned us about judging and with the measure we use, it will be measured back to us (Matt. 7:1-6).

Our greatest enemy is self – self that has not surrendered to God – we have not offered our bodies as 'living sacrifices' which is merely our reasonable service (Romans 12:1), nor taken up our cross daily and followed the Master. All too often it is not, 'Thy will be done,' but *my will* be done. The apostle Paul wrote: 'He [Jesus] died for all, that those who live should no longer live for themselves, but for Him who died for them and rose again' (2 Corinthians 5:15). Self must be crucified and dethroned.

'For I through the law died to the law that I might live to God. I have been crucified with Christ; it is no longer I who live, but Christ lives in me; and the life which I now live in the flesh I live by faith in the Son of God, who loved me and gave Himself for me' (Galatians 2:19-20). We are not our own, as we have been bought at a great price and should glorify God through our surrendered lives (1 Corinthians 6:19-20).

If you confess that Jesus Christ is Lord then you must allow Him to be in *full* control, to be led of the Holy Spirit. Full and unconditional surrender to the will of God; putting to death the old man and exchanging your life for His; a giving of yourself to be entirely at His disposal, and to hate the things of the world, so that they have no hold over you (1 John 2:15-17). So that you can live entirely for the glory of God and to be led of the Holy Spirit.

The apostle Paul wrote: '…Shall we continue in sin that grace may abound? Certainly not! How shall we who died to sin live any longer in it? Or do you not know that as many of us as were baptised in Christ Jesus were baptised into His death? Therefore, we were buried with Him through baptism into death, that just as Christ was raised from the dead by the glory of the Father, even so *we also should walk in newness of life.* For if we have been united together in the likeness of His death, certainly we also shall be in the likeness of His resurrection, knowing this, that the old man was crucified with Him, that the body of sin might be done away with, that we should no longer be slaves of sin' (Romans 6:1-6).

'Beloved, I beg you as sojourners and pilgrims, abstain from fleshly lusts which war against the soul, having your conduct honourable among the Gentiles that when they speak against you as evildoers, they may, by your good works which they observe, glorify God in the day of visitation' (1 Peter 2:11-12).

Chapter 11

Sluice Gate, Sin and Contempt

'Be sober, be vigilant; because your adversary the devil walks about like a roaring lion, seeking whom he may devour. Resist him steadfast in the faith...' (1 Peter 5:8-9).

The Enemy has his Hooks in Many of My People
(The Bait of Satan, Outside of My Shoal of Protection)

This is what the Sovereign Lord says,

"The enemy has his hooks in many of My people and they have become snared. They have taken the bait of Satan and have been lured away to swim outside of My shoal of protection, and there has been compromise. But, in My goodness and mercy, I opened up a sluice for those who were willing to swim through, but that sluice is now slowly closing to those who are deliberately disobedient.[1] There are no lengths to which I will not go, to warn those who have chosen to swim with the spirit who is now at work in those who are disobedient.[2]

"Today, there are many with an independent spirit who chose their will over Mine and refuse the way of their Saviour. Many (not all) have gone out or have been sent out in My name as fishers of men, but now, I am reeling some of them in and will separate the good fish from the bad. Some will be placed to one side and taught further truth, because it is by the truth you can be set free. Some will be thrown back as unsuitable and a few will come to an end. Many are self deluded, influenced by deceiving spirits and are a burden to others, and a danger to themselves as well as others.

"There is no place in My River of Life for those with an independent spirit, who believe what they want to believe and put their own spin or interpretation on what My Holy Spirit says to them. As I called forth My Son to lay His life down, so I have called others. This is not some form of theoretical death, but a daily dying to self so that My Holy Spirit can accomplish His work here and now on the earth."

Michael Backholer, 14 Sept. 2009 – www.ProphecyNow.co.uk

* 1. 'For it is shameful even to mention what the disobedient do in secret' (Ephesians 5:12), NIV.
* 2. 'In which you used to live when you followed the ways of this world and of the ruler of the kingdom of the air, the spirit who is now at work in those who are disobedient' (Ephesians 2:2), NIV.

ILAWA.

Mercy Triumphs Over Judgment
(Justice Must be Seen to Run its Course)

The following was revealed in the secret place of prayer over a period of time in September 2009.

There is no such thing as cheap grace and justice must be seen to run its course.

Little or no effort is required to walk through an open door, but to climb through a window calls for real effort; depending on the size and height of the window, and each window is tailor-made.

The sins of the fathers fall on the children to the third and fourth generations of those who hate God; and Satan, knowing his time to be short, driven by his inflamed hatred for the Body of Christ, set into motion an extreme onslaught, to derail the gospel being preached to all the nations in the twentieth century. But the Lord God in all His sovereignty opened a window of extraordinary grace to enable those who wish, to enter and avail themselves of this time of unmerited favour.

Now in the twenty-first century this window is slowly closing to those who are an offence to the Lord God. Sin has been allowed to run its course as an act of judgment.[3]

'There is a way that seems right to a man but in the end it leads to death' (Proverbs 14:12).

Michael Backholer, 16 Sept. 2009 – www.ProphecyNow.co.uk

- 3. 'Therefore God gave them over in the sinful desires of their hearts to sexual impurity for the degrading of their bodies with one another' (Romans 1:24), NIV.
- 'But because of your stubbornness and your unrepentant heart, you are storing up wrath against yourself for the day of God's wrath, when His righteous judgment will be revealed. God will give to each person according to what He has done. To those who by persistence in doing good seek glory, honour and immortality, He will give eternal life. But for those who are self-seeking and who reject the truth and follow evil, there will be wrath and anger' (Romans 2:5-8), NIV.
- 'But My people would not listen to Me; Israel would not submit to Me. So I gave them over to their stubborn heart to follow their own devices' (Psalm 81:11-12), NIV.

For further reading and study: 1 Corinthians 6:9-11, Galatians 5:19-21, Ephesians 5:3-7, Philippians 3:17-19, Revelation 9:20-21 and Revelation 21:8.

In the twentieth century, the First World War (1914-1918), saw more than ten million people killed, whilst the consequences of World War II (1939-1945), saw a minimum of fifty million dead (with some historians stating the figure to be as high as seventy million). Millions were killed before their time. These are signs of the last days[4] and the end of the age, before the glorious return of Jesus Christ, who is coming back for a pure and spotless Bride.

- 4. There will be false Christ's, false prophets, tribulation, persecution, betrayals, martyrdoms, famines, earthquakes, pestilence, wars, rumours of wars, troubles, fearful sights, great signs from Heaven, and because of lawlessness, the love of many will grow cold. See Matthew 24, Mark 13 and Luke 21.

- 'Behold the eyes of the Lord is on those who fear Him, on those who hope in mercy' (Psalm 33:18).
- 'The fear of the Lord is the beginning of knowledge' (Proverbs 1:7a). See also Proverbs 9:10 and Luke 12:5.
- 'The fear of the Lord is to hate evil' (Proverbs 8:13a).

Forewarned is Forearmed
(The Fear of the Lord is the Beginning of Knowledge)

This is what the Sovereign Lord says,

"Overfamiliarity has bred contempt. In these last generations, there has been a cataclysmic shift in the attitude of many towards My Holy Spirit. Many have become impertinent and disobedient and habitually rationalise (justify by plausible reasoning) the truth of My Word, and the leadings of My Holy Spirit and therefore grieve Him immensely. Far too many operate independently of Him in My name and this will not be tolerated, as I prepare to pour out My Spirit in greater abundance in these last generations.

"Therefore, greater persecution will also arise, so it is expedient at this time that I call forth My prophets from their hidden places to thunder out My message of warning. Do not be deceived, a time is coming when those who ignore My Holy Spirit will do so at their own peril, because the battle will become so fierce at times, that many who have chosen not to be one with Him are not one with Us (Father and Son). Yet, for your encouragement, I would remind you that you are indeed one of the most privileged generations, if you embrace Him wholeheartedly and My Word of truth.

"Many in this generation enjoyed singing the words of the song, 'In Heavenly armour.' Truly I say to you, that the end-time battle truly does belong to the Lord, and those who have chosen not to be one with My Holy Spirit will not stand, but fall when the battle is at its fiercest.

"I am a holy God, a Consuming Fire, so do not be deceived into thinking – as some have been taught – that you can approach Me as your mate or buddy. The fear of the Lord is the beginning of knowledge, and only those with clean hands and a pure heart can ascend the hill of the Lord, and stand in the holy place. For without holiness, no one will see Me."

Michael Backholer, 28 Sept. 2009 – www.ProphecyNow.co.uk

'Cry aloud, spare not; lift up your voice...tell My people their transgression and the house of Jacob their sins' (Isaiah 58:1).

Chapter 12

The Climate and End-Times

'For the earth will be filled with the knowledge of the glory of the Lord, as the waters cover the sea' (Habakkuk 2:14).

Global Warming, Global Warning and the Glory Season (Concern Yourselves with the Effect of My Son)

This is what the Sovereign Lord says,

"There was a time when mankind had only one language, one speech, yet in their heart they decided to make a name for themselves irrespective of the cost. So it is today, man continues to struggle and strive to be noticed above all others. Yet I say to you, there is but One name that is above all others, a name that is Wonderful, Magnificent, Almighty and worthy of man's praise and adoration – that name is Jesus.

"This is the name given to mankind by which they can be saved from sin – salvation is found in no other. This is the name that multitudes refused to deny and died for. Let those who have ears hear and take note.

"There are seasons, and many say this is a season of global warming, but I say to you, if I were to speak the word, a cool breeze would come upon the earth and all that would change, for nothing is too difficult for Me. But I say to you, be watchful for a season of glory, a season that will bring glory to My Son, as well as Myself has begun. In this glory season, millions upon millions will turn from their sin to My Son, Jesus Christ the Messiah. Do not be over concerned with the effect of the sun, but concern yourselves with the effect of My Son. For He is the only One that can save you from your sins and all that will come upon the earth."

Michael Backholer, 1 March 2007 – www.ProphecyNow.co.uk

'Surely His salvation is near those who fear Him, that glory may dwell in the land' (Psalm 85:10).

The Economic Climate
(And a Look at the Church)

This is what the Sovereign Lord says,

"I hear the sound of voices all over the world, people who are anxious, fearful and some who are distraught. A people who have lost hope, a people who do not know Me or know of My love, listening, watching, thinking and asking, 'Who can we put our trust in now? Who can we believe? What is the world coming to? Will this ever end?' All the lies, the deceit, the deception; bankers, politicians and leaders saying one thing one day and then later doing another. Where is it all leading? Some say this is the hand of God at work, sifting and shaking, a sign of Divine displeasure.

"Some are looking to the Church for an anchor and direction – what will they find? What will they see? What will they hear? Will they find faith? True hope? A house of prayer for all nations? A refuge? A place of blessing where My will on earth is done as in Heaven? – Full of loving, forgiving people. A place where My Holy Spirit is welcome and moving in power. Convicting, converting, delivering and healing or will they find that a partial darkness has settled and replaced the light that calls itself the Church, a reflection of the world?"

Michael Backholer, 2 March 2009 – www.ProphecyNow.co.uk

Jesus, in relation to the end-times said, "And you will hear of wars and rumour of wars. See that you are not troubled; for all these things must come to pass, but the end is not yet. For nation will rise against nation, and kingdom against kingdom. And there will be famines, pestilences, and earthquakes in various places. All these are the beginning of sorrows." (Matthew 24:6-8).

Jesus said, "Do not lay up for yourselves treasures on earth, where moth and rust destroy and where thieves break in and steal; but lay up for yourselves treasures in Heaven, where neither moth nor rust destroys and thieves do not break in and steal. For where your treasure is, there your heart will be also" (Matthew 6:19-21).

Jews and Gentiles Coming Together as One
(Israel and Revival – The End-Times)

This is what the Sovereign Lord says,

"Behold, says the Lord God of Israel, behold, I AM the God of Abraham, the God of Isaac and the God of Jacob, and I declare that I AM rich in mercy and full of compassion towards My people. Behold, says the Lord, you have seen the first fruits of the two becoming one, but now, says the Lord God of all the earth, a time is coming, and soon to be upon you, when I will pour out My Spirit in Israel, as in the beginning, and all that was foretold will come to pass, and all those in Israel who are truly Mine will arise.

"As My Spirit and My fire comes upon them, then an irruption will take place throughout the earth, as the two truly become one, and work together in true love in the unity of My Spirit, through the bond of peace in the power of My Holy Spirit for My glory."

Michael Backholer, 11 Oct. 2009 – www.ProphecyNow.co.uk

The apostle Paul wrote: 'I say then, has God cast away His people? Certainly not! For I am also am an Israelite of the seed of Abraham, of the tribe of Benjamin. God has not cast away His people whom He foreknew.... Even so then, at this present time there is a remnant according to the election of grace.... For if you were cut out of the olive tree which is wild by nature and were grafted contrary to nature into a good olive tree, how much more will these, who are the natural branches, be grafted into their own olive tree? For I do not desire, brethren, that you should be ignorant of this mystery, lest you should be wise in your own opinion, that hardening in part has happened to Israel until the fullness of the Gentiles has come in. And so all Israel will be saved as it is written: 'The Deliverer will come out of Zion, and He will turn away ungodliness from Jacob; for this is My covenant with them, when I take away their sins' ' (Romans 11:1-2, 5-6, 24-27). See also Zechariah 14:3-4 and Acts 1:6-7.

Chapter 13

The Church and Her Issues

Jesus said, "Not everyone who says to Me, 'Lord, Lord,' shall enter the Kingdom of Heaven, but he who does the will of My Father in Heaven" (Matthew 7:21).

The True and the False Church
(Produce Fruit)

This is what the Sovereign Lord says,

"Just as a fog of lies, deceit and deception entered the garden in the beginning, so the same fog of deception has been cultivated in the minds of many in the Church. There are those who are living under false pretences and claim to be a part of the Church. However, this is a charade, a deception, an abomination in My sight. Their fruit is a projected delusion and rotten to the core. On the surface to the untrained eye and the undiscerning, it looks appetising, but on closer inspection, it is found to be counterfeit. Just like the waxed and plastic fruit, it is *all* for show.

"But know this, I am dissecting all that is false and am gifting that which is true, to discern and know the difference. There is a Spirit of Truth and a spirit of falsehood, the true gospel and a false gospel, true apostles and false apostles, a true anointing and a counterfeit anointing. And yes, there are true prophets and false prophets – and by their fruit will you recognise them. For that which is true will produce lasting fruit, fruit of the light, true fruit of My Spirit.

"Avoid the fruitless deeds of darkness and produce fruit in keeping with repentance. Therefore, repent for all your fruitless deeds of darkness while there is still time, because My fire is coming on My Church, to test the true quality of each man's fruit and his works."

Michael Backholer, 8 Nov. 2009 – www.ProphecyNow.co.uk

Ambassadors for Christ
(Do I have your Attention?)

This is what the Sovereign Lord says,

"To all those who would still claim to be ambassadors of the Lord Jesus Christ, I say to you, what on earth are you doing? There is no higher calling than to be called to represent My Son and His name, which is above every other. Tell me, what do I have to do to get your attention? Be warned there are no lengths to which I will not go to secure your attention. Whatever it takes, I will get it and lay hold of you.

"Those of you who choose to continue on aimlessly as if I have not spoken to you are in for a real shock. Do not delude yourselves into thinking because you have done this, that or the other in My Son's name, that somehow you still have Our approval. For I say to you, that your way of doing things is not necessarily Our ways, and are in truth, often a hindrance to what you have been called to do. Why are so many so reluctant to listen to what We have been saying to you? Do you not have ears to hear? Have you not read all that was written down as a warning for all on whom the fulfilment of this age has come? No one should think that they are special or indispensable, no matter how big or small, you, or others believe your ministry to be.

"Ask yourself, are you truly in My will being led of My Spirit? Do not make the mistake of thinking that somehow I deal differently with you than all the others. Consider carefully those who went before you, as I do not have any favourites. But some are more at one with My Holy Spirit and learnt the true meaning of abiding in Me.

"You say you are called, chosen and sent – but I would ask you, by whom? For you are not doing as I asked, nor are you listening to My Holy Spirit. So, I would remind you, if I was able to catch David's and Jonah's attention, then surely I can get yours also, but for some it will be too late. I have got the attention of many through their economies, and many sat up and took notice when their planes were grounded.

"You are about to enter into a time of great difficulties that many have never experienced and are in no position to avoid. If

I do not have your full attention at this time, you will suffer needlessly. So I say again, do not believe in your hearts that you are somehow special or different to the others, and that I do things differently with you. I have got Netanhyahu's attention and I will get Obama's also. I have got the attention of a few of what you consider to be the larger Christian ministries, but it has cost some of them profoundly.

"As the governments of the world slip and slide towards a new order, I too, am bringing My order to My Church. So I say to you, repent and turn back to Me while there is still time."

Michael Backholer, 29 April 2010 – www.ProphecyNow.co.uk

God's love for mankind is immense and is documented in the most famous verse of the Holy Bible, John 3:16, 'For God so loved the world that He gave His only begotten Son, that whoever believes in Him should not perish but have everlasting life' (John 3:16).

The disciples were commissioned to preach and teach about the Kingdom of God; to proclaim the good news of salvation, to make disciples, to cast out demons, to heal the sick and raise the dead (Matthew 28:18-20 and Mark 16:15-18) – all in the mighty name of Jesus Christ. These commands of Jesus Christ are just as binding to us today, as to the early disciples to whom Jesus spoke. They are passed from one generation to the next until every tribe and tongue has heard the glad tidings, 'as a witness to all nations' and then, and only then, will Jesus come again (Matthew 24:14, Revelation 5:9 and Revelation 7:9). However, remember that Peter in relation to the Day of the Lord (the end-times), reiterated that we have our part to play – our responsibility and duty towards mankind. God is 'longsuffering towards us, not willing that any should perish but that all should come to repentance' and that we should be 'looking for and hastening the coming of the day of God' (2 Peter 3:9-12). This is when we fulfil our vital role in the Great Commission by personal evangelism, and aiding overseas outreach: practically, financially and prayerfully – go, give, pray! We all need an anointing from God, the baptism of the Holy Spirit (Luke 24:49 & Acts 1:5, 8). If the Church does not evangelise, it will fossilise! "I am the Lord, and besides Me there is no Saviour...you are My witnesses..." (Isa. 43:11-12).

Burdened, the Shadows of Darkness and Mercy
(Walk in the Light)

This is what the Sovereign Lord says,

"Many, yes many in this hour who truly believe all that is written in My Word are also truly perplexed. I hear their silent groans coming from deep within them, as deep calls to deep, spirit to Spirit. 'O Lord,' they cry out, 'O God,' they cry out, 'O Lord my God,' is the cry of their hearts. 'When, Lord God,' they ask? 'When? How much longer must we wait, why, why, why do You stay Your hand?' [Why do You not intervene and do something?]. 'How much longer must we wait?'

"Many feel ripped and torn deep within their souls as they rend their hearts to Me. Day and night they cry out. Wounded hearts, begging, pleading, crying out, 'In Your anger remember mercy,' and yes sadly, I hear others whose hearts have become hardened and are not one at heart with their Saviour, Jesus Christ of Nazareth, who is sat at My right hand interceding for them. Yet they call out for judgment on any or anything they disapprove of. But as all these cries are filtered and cleansed through My Son and the blood that He shed for all mankind on Calvary, I hear the sweet sound of My Holy Spirit who intercedes Himself, with groans that mere words cannot express. For He intercedes according to My will and it is My will to pour out My Spirit on all people, all flesh. But as in all generations, I see religious umbrellas going up from hearts that have become hardened by sin which grieves, yes grieves My Holy Spirit.

"Listen, listen, for I share with you this day a mystery – not all welcomed My Holy Spirit on the Day of Pentecost, but those that did were empowered, gifted and went out and turned the world upside down! But many of you have spent so much time flirting and prostituting yourselves with the world, that you are walking in the shadows of darkness of your own sinful nature and the ways of the world.

"Even now, as My Spirit is poured out it cascades all around you, so I call you to walk in the light as I am in the light, for you know not by what manner of spirit that you cry out to Me. The Son came to seek and to save all that were lost, not to destroy them. So repent and be forgiven, for the measure you use, will be measured to you also."

Michael Backholer, 10 May 2010 – www.ProphecyNow.co.uk

'Their heart cried out to the Lord, "O wall of the daughter of Zion, let tears run down like a river day and night; give yourself no relief; give your eyes no rest. Arise, cry out in the night, at the beginning of the watches; pour out your heart like water before the face of the Lord. Lift your hands towards Him for the life of your young children..." ' (Lamentations 2:18-19).

The Church Pendulum is out of Alignment
(It is not Swinging True to My Word or Will)

This is what the Sovereign Lord says,

"Look, listen, concentrate, focus – do you see it? Do you hear it? What is it you say? It's not a small still voice I hear, nor is it the sound of a great powerful wind that tears mountains apart and shatters rock. It's more than a whisper and far more dangerous than rocks shattering. You will only see it, hear it, if you are in close fellowship, true fellowship with My Holy Spirit. It's not momentary, no, far from it and it is far more serious. It has become long lasting and in some places permanent. In some parts of the world it has become the norm and so deep rooted and blatant that the people of this world can see it, discern it. So why is it that those who have eyes to see and ears to hear cannot?

"Tick-tock, tick-tock, tick-tock, tick, tick-tock, tick-tock, tick-tock, tick. There it is, that's it! It's the pendulum at the heart of the Church clock. It's not swinging true to My Word or will, it's out of alignment, out of balance. If this was Big Ben [in London, England] that needed to be corrected, they would use a small coin. But it will take more than money to realign the Church. Money is not the solution and it is in fact part of the problem. This has not happened due to normal wear and tear, no, this has come about due to neglect.

"This is more than a few dry cogs needing greasing or the mechanism needing some slight adjustment. For some it will mean a complete spiritual strip down and overhaul. A cleansing and the anointing oil of My Holy Spirit in order that She keeps in time with Me, My Word and My will. It is going to take much more than a spring-clean to remove the rubbish and dirt that has become so ingrained that many believe it to be part of the workings.

"There was a time when the people would listen out for Her chimes but not anymore, they turn their heads and close their ears. So it is to you who have ears to hear and eyes to see, I say open them and ask yourself, does this ring true to you?"

Michael Backholer, 13 May 2010 – www.ProphecyNow.co.uk

Shortage of Good Fruit
(Bacteria Abides in the Church)

This is what the Sovereign Lord says,

"It is written: 'Man does not live on bread alone, but on every word that comes from the mouth of the Lord,' however, many in this hour only exist on a few crumbs that fall from the Master's table. While others try to survive on the endless supply of junk food which has little or nothing to do with the true Word of God.

"To be strong, healthy and fit for purpose the human body must be nourished, exercised and rested. The human spirit must also be fed and nourished with the healthy diet of God's Word. If either is neglected and you receive a poor or inadequate diet, or have poor hygiene, in time there will be inevitable problems and prevention is more preferable than cure. Good personal hygiene is also imperative to maintain a strong healthy body free of disease and infection.

"It is also written, 'Thus by their fruit you will recognise them,' and 'The acts of sinful nature are obvious.' So I will bring to your attention what by now should be obvious to all in the Body of Christ. The gifts of My Spirit are freely given, but the fruit of My Spirit, like the fruit of the vine takes time to grow from the moment you are grafted into the Vine by rebirth, receiving My Spirit as a deposit of what is to come. My Spirit continually nurtures fruit, true fruit; good fruit that shows you are My disciples which bring glory to the Father. Likewise, fruit bearing branches are pruned back to encourage new growth and thus become even more fruitful. Branches that are diseased, sterile and unable or unwilling to produce fruit are cut out and burned.

"Sadly, in this generation there is a shortage of good fruit, true fruit and parts of the Vine (Body of Christ) have become wounded, and the wounds have become infected with disease. Sadly the wounds have been neglected and festered, and the antiseptic balm of forgiveness has not been applied to prevent further infection spreading to other parts of the Body. There are sores and boils that are full of pus and poisoning My Body.

"It is plain for all to see that My Body, the Body of Christ is far from pure and bacteria abides. I have no choice but to lance these boils to drain away all the impurities. This will be a very uncomfortable process but necessary. Then I shall be able to pour out and apply the antibiotic and resurrection power of My Holy Spirit to reinvigorate, and revive My Body, the Church."

Michael Backholer, 6 August 2010 – www.ProphecyNow.co.uk

Jesus said, "Take heed that no one deceives you..." (Matthew 13:5), and those who say that they cannot be deceived, already are! Also, not all signs and miracles are from God. Jesus said, "For false christs and false prophets will arise and show great signs and wonders, so as to deceive, if possible, even the elect" (Matthew 24:4-5, 24 and Mark 13:22-23). The apostle Paul wrote: 'I fear, less somehow, as the serpent deceived Eve by his craftiness, so your minds may be corrupted from the simplicity that is in Christ,' by those who preach another Jesus, another gospel and who have a different spirit (2 Corinthians 11:3-4).

Satan has many followers infiltrating churches, false apostles and false teachers (2 Corinthians 11:13-15). There are also those who will deny the power of God, even in the day of visitation (2 Timothy 3:1-9). Whilst some so-called 'believers' are known as tares, wolves or accursed children (Matthew 7:15, Matthew 13:24-30 and 2 Peter 2:14-15). Jesus warned of false prophets who will come in sheep's clothing, but inwardly they are ravenous wolves. By their fruits we will know them (Matthew 7:15-20). Jesus also said, "If you abide in My Word, you are My disciples indeed. And you shall know the truth, and the truth shall make you free" (John 8:31-32).

Chapter 14

Offensive Christian Workers

Jesus said, "I tell you, I do not know you, where you are from. Depart from Me, all you workers of iniquity" (Luke 13:27).

A Word for the Few in the Body of Christ
(Fleecing My People – Professional Fundraisers)

This is what the Sovereign Lord says,

"Enough is enough; no longer will I suffer or tolerate ministers and ministries who operate in My name and fleece, yes, fleece My people. You manipulate them and prey on their emotions to part with their hard-earned income. You say it is for My Kingdom and promise them blessings in My name, which I have not spoken to you. Furthermore, you twist and distort My Word to fit in with your own evil schemes. And I tell you, not only will I call you to give an account of every word you have falsely spoken in My name to millions, yes millions, who have put their trust in you, in the false hope that their giving 'now' would deliver them. And then what do you do? You have the presumption to throw it back into their face and call it faith, as you boast of your wealth and parade before them your gold and silver, and all your trappings of a materialistic lifestyle. Do not be deceived, you shall reap what you have sown. I give you fair warning, repent while there is still time.

"How dare you employ professional fundraisers who have the audacity to stand and say they are men of God, and My people should trust them. Think long and hard about this, for I shall release My Spirit that will quicken My people to discern what you are up to; then we shall see if your faith is truly in the Lord your God. Furthermore, if you were to practice what you preach, there would be no need to continually bombard My people with your false claims, the voice of the Lord has spoken, take heed."

Michael Backholer, 15 Feb. 2006 – www.ProphecyNow.co.uk

Pockets with Holes – Are you Doing God's Will?
(Do you Desire YOUR will over Mine? – Squandering £$€)

This is what the Sovereign Lord says,

"What have you done with My gospel? What are you doing in My name? I told you to go and make disciples and teach them all that I commanded – deny yourself, carry your cross and follow Me. The ones who truly love Me share in My sufferings when called to, without complaining and still manage to obey My teaching. What kind of example are you setting? And by what authority do you do the things you do?

"Next year, yes, next year, I will have your attention, your whole attention, your undivided attention. One way or another you will be compelled to be still and take stock of all that you do in My name. I have sent you wise men and women, prophets and intercessors to warn you, guide you and bring you back in line with My will and My Word. But you would not listen, you refused to heed My warnings.

"Listen to the voice of the Lord, next year, yes, next year; I will command your attention. I will touch you where it hurts and stop you dead in your tracks. You cannot go on as you have, and I will not permit you to. You think My pockets are deep and so they are, but yours are full of holes. How deep are your pockets and your pride? I ask, for I intend to show you and touch them both, and if you dare to continue to refuse to acknowledge the true state of both and repent, you will be called to step aside or even stand down, so the ones whom I have called and chosen can complete the work, in keeping with My will and Word.

"You cannot carry on as you have with pride in your hearts, somehow believing that you are special or different to all the others, when in fact, some are strangers to My Holy Spirit and yet claim to be led by Him. So it is with those who claim to be My disciples, yet desire their will over Mine, and call for more and more to squander on themselves, and their own ideas. I say again, next year your pockets will not be stretched as your income shrinks, but know this: I shall provide for all those I have called and chosen, and set apart to complete the Every Creature Commission, and they shall go forth in the power of

My Spirit in keeping with the intercessions of My little flock, once in Swansea."[1]

Michael Backholer, 29 June 2010 – www.ProphecyNow.co.uk

1. This is a reference to the legacy of the intercessions gained by the Holy Spirit through Rees Howells and the team of intercessors at the Bible College of Wales during the 1930s and 40s and then under Samuel Rees Howells from the 1950s onwards; he died in March 2004. See www.ReesHowells.co.uk.

Are you IN Christ? The Hill of the Lord
(Tinsel Ministries and Celebrity City)

This is what the Sovereign Lord says,

"Let it be known that there are men and women whose soul desire is to worship Me in Spirit and in truth. They are devoted to Me and their devotion keeps them in My presence, they are not My servants but My friends. I laid down My life for them and they have chosen to lay down their lives for Me. They have nothing that they can truly call their own and lay no claim to anything, except the claim I have on their lives.

"They have no titles or well publicised ministries, neither do they seek them in this hour of carnal carnivals, with all its self-promotion. They have left the wanderings of the wilderness with its dark night of the soul. They have finished groping about in the fog, in the Valley of Indecision long ago and climbed the Hill of the Lord. They have turned their backs on the bright lights of Celebrity City, and seen through the call for more and more money to prop up the bright lights ministries with all its tinsel.

"In every generation there are the few, the hidden ones who have died to self, died to the world, they have nothing to prove and no one to impress. They can be found daily greeting Me around the clock, around the world, anticipating the small still voice of My Spirit. These are the ones that know My voice and the power of a holy life, and truly are My friends. Channels who are willing and able to serve Me, and carry out My will. Like the angels, few see them, but their service is indispensable and beyond the comprehension of many in the Church today. You may know them by name and consider them a little odd or even over the top at times, but care not of such things. They are overcomers who when called to bind the strong man, tear down strongholds and cast mountains into the sea at My command. "They are not impressed with the brash claims of some who rant and rave about their so called exploits – all this is abhorrent to them and to Me. Consider carefully your own position for I ask, are you truly in Christ? For many operate under a different spirit and one day they will be shocked into knowing that I am a complete stranger to them. The oil of My anointing will mix with living water but never with that which is polluted. There is no place in My house for worldly wisdom and it is imperative that you discern and decide your own position, for it is your choice and if you lack wisdom, true wisdom, all you have to do is ask."

Michael Backholer, 22 Aug. 2010 – www.ProphecyNow.co.uk

God's Vineyard
(New Wine or Vinegar – True Worship)

This is what the Sovereign Lord says,

"Something different has taken root in parts of My vineyard. Some are enthusiastic to cultivate it and propagate more from this rootstock[2] while others are unsure of its roots and origin. True, there are no signs of black spot, rust or mildew, but this is not a Rose of Sharon. On closer examination, you will discover there are suckers originating from below the graft, below the surface. If they are not removed the whole plant will backslide, oh yes, there is vigorous growth and so it is with the rootstock of the dog rose that grows wild amongst the weeds. But this resembles a brier, a thorn bush that will never produce a good vintage. Do people pick grapes from thorn bushes? This is indeed a tare, illegitimate and unholy from the root up, and cannot be grafted into the True Vine. There are great proclamations made about it and exuberant claims, and celebrations taking place – but this is not the sign of a great harvest, but these are signs of a people clowning around without any restraint or self-control. This has all the hallmarks of a circus. Look at the fruit I say, or should I say look for the fruit. This is of the flesh and will never mature into new wine and is only fit for vinegar. [C.f. Amos 5:21-24 and Malachi 1:6-14].

"There is nothing new under the sun. Even David, a man after My own heart loved to worship and celebrate before Me with all his might. He would dance and leap for joy with great exuberance, but was despised by some, but he could not help himself for his love for Me welled up within him and gushed forth in wonder and adoration. Unlike so many today, in this feel good circus of entertainment that is currently doing the rounds of My vineyard.

"Have you never read about the time when Jesus was full of joy through the Holy Spirit? It is for this reason I also ask, where is all your joy emanating from? And more to the point, is this truly worship? So I ask again, when you come together to whoopee, is it really for Me? Or is it just something you do for yourselves? What of the rest of the week when you are alone, do you dance the same for Me then? Or is it just part of the show when you come together in My name. By the way, David would dance daily and while alone. Consider this and meditate on it for there are those who are too frail to join in and be a part of this outward boisterous merrymaking. Yet daily, yes, daily I say, they dance for Me deep within their souls and worship Me in Spirit and in truth, deep within their hearts. I love to see My people worship and celebrate in all the diversity of their cultures. But you must learn to discern between that which is of My Spirit and that which is of your flesh, before the love of most grows cold."

Michael Backholer, 16 Sept. 2010 – www.ProphecyNow.co.uk

2. This prophecy relates to God as the Great Gardener and has specific meaning to those familiar with horticulture – the cultivation of plants, John 15:1-11.

'The Spirit of the Lord is upon Me because the Lord has anointed Me to preach good tidings to the poor... To comfort those who mourn in Zion, to give them beauty for ashes, the oil of joy for mourning, the garment of praise for the spirit of heaviness; that they may be called trees of righteousness, the planting of the Lord, that He may be glorified' (Isaiah 61:1a, 3).

The True Light Versus Religious Celebrations & Traditions
(Presumption and its Consequences)

This is what the Sovereign Lord says,

"Moses My servant warned the people in the wilderness about the sin of presumption and of the consequences (Numbers 14). My servant David also knew it to be a great transgression (Psalm 19:13), and so it came to pass, as I surveyed the timeline along the road of the fullness of time, from alpha to omega; I glanced upon My people trimming trees. There was wonder and excitement, a time of feasting and festivity celebrating the birth of Jesus. There were lights twinkling all over the trees.

"At the base of the trees there were some presents, some were books that had been written about My Son, My Spirit and Myself. There was another Book that remained the bestseller but only a few glanced at it from time to time, and fewer still spent the time to read and study it, preferring to read the others. The greater number of lights at the bottom of the tree were looking to the few at the top, to shed more light on the bestseller, but they were unable to. Oh yes, they knew that the Book held the truth about the Light of the World, but sadly many of them had never truly entered into the light and were a shadow of the truth, and still in partial darkness themselves, are unable to share the light with others who looked up to them.

"Untold numbers had been deceived and were living in the shadow of the Truth under the branch of religious tradition. They celebrated and feasted, but would refuse to attend the wedding banquet that had been prepared, and chose to continue down another road that was aptly named, 'The Rules and Traditions of Men.' It was most popular and very busy. There were other roads and avenues of distraction, but they all converged at the road of The Cross where it narrowed and continued through the Valley of Decision. This was illuminated by the Light of the World that was nailed to a tree on the hill, overlooking all of creation. 'So since the creation of the world God's invisible and Divine nature – have been clearly seen, being understood from what has been made, so that men are without excuse' (Romans 1:20), NIV.

"In the last days, My people began to place more and more lights, baubles and all manner of trimmings on their trees to attract others, believing it to be more user friendly and less offensive. Had they spent the time and read the bestseller they would have know that the Light of the World was sent to be an offence to the darkness, and overcome it. So it was, that presumption entered the hearts and minds of many, and they believed that they had the power and energy required to bring the Light to all the world. And in their presumption they came up with a never-ending supply of bright ideas that caused many to become dull, as they slithered further and further from the Tree of Life and the right to eat from it. As the road neared its end, the wise who had oil in their jars, as well as their lamps, went into the wedding banquet while others whom appeared at one time to be bright sparks went off to buy oil."

Michael Backholer, 16 Feb. 2011 – www.ProphecyNow.co.uk

Jesus learned obedience through His suffering, as did Paul and all the other apostles. Many today repel discipline and suffering, yet willingly embrace denominational denial of biblical truth. Even Barnabas was led astray for a time in his day. The enthusiasm of the flesh knows no bounds, encouraged as it is by the sinful self-nature of the flesh. That which is not crucified under the direction of the Holy Spirit will lead many into self-deception and delusion, believing that they can take or win whole towns, cities and nations without the leading or direction of the Holy Spirit. (See The Lord's Paratroopers, chapter 16).

We should not build our biblical knowledge or faith on one truth, only to neglect other truths which are equally important. We can overemphasise or give more prominence to some issues and neglect or underemphasise others. If you take just one part of truth and do not consider the other parts, then you will reach a wrong conclusion. Truth out of balance becomes error. There is truth, half truth and error. Truth is found in having firm grounding in the Word of God. Half truth and error can be because of ignorance (Acts 18:24-26), deception (2 Timothy 3:13) or being under the influence of deceiving spirits (1 Timothy 4:1-2). Read *and apply* the truths of the Holy Bible (James 1:22), 'the whole counsel of God' (Acts 20:27).

Infants or Disciples – Nations Shaking
(Shaking their Finances and their Beliefs)

This is what the Sovereign Lord says,

"It is written that Jesus Christ the Son of God was born of a woman, wrapped in swaddling clothes and placed in a manger. So I ask, where were you placed when you were born? In a cradle to be rocked to sleep, then to waken with the cries of, 'Feed me! Feed me!' Then to be fed and comforted with all your needs met. So I ask, when you were born again, where were you placed? In the cradle of a church building to be rocked back and forth as mere infants in Christ? Why are you still crying out for milk? Wake up, get up and sit at My table and have your fill of solid food.

"Why are so many who claim to be My disciples still in diapers (nappies), being fed by a wet nurse? It was never My will or intention for the multitudes to be cradled behind four walls and exist on milk. Milk is for infants, solid food is for the mature who have trained themselves in righteousness and know the difference between good and evil. Wake up! Get up! And grow up!

"I am shaking the nations, their finances and their beliefs, while you become more and more spiritually obese on a diet of fleshly sermons that nurture self and self-will. Get up and open your eyes and you will see the beginning of the birth pains that Jesus warned about. The earth is groaning as if in labour, My Spirit is groaning, yet you continue to sleep on in the cradle of your own comfort zone. There is a time and a place of great darkness, weeping and gnashing of teeth, so let your light shine forth, now for all to see outside the four walls of your cradle of preference.

"I am full of compassion and mercy, go forth, go out while there is still time. The harvest is plentiful, but the workers are few. Go I say, go and tell the people the good news of the life, death and resurrection of Jesus Christ. Tell them of the cross and the blood – what are you waiting for? For them to come to you? Or Jesus' return?"

Michael Backholer, 2 April 2011 – www.ProphecyNow.co.uk

Chapter 15

Unholy Gain and Financial Manipulation

'The love of money is a root of all kinds of evil, for some have strayed from the faith in their greediness, and pierced themselves through with many sorrows. But you, O man of God, flee these things and pursue righteousness, godliness, faith, love, patience, gentleness. Fight the good fight of faith, lay hold on eternal life, to which you were called...' (1 Timothy 6:10-12).

Sold Out For Jesus or Selling Him?
(Unholy Beggars who Fleece the Bride)

This is what the Sovereign Lord says,

"Judas sold Jesus for 30 pieces of silver, the Roman soldiers flogged Him and few today are truly sold out to Him; whilst others have no qualms of selling Him short in all their dealings with others in His name. Many I say, many have peddled My grace and devalued it and cheapened the gospel to a knock down bottom price. The true price of the cross and the blood of Christ has been dragged down and down to the bargain bottom basement. Riches and wealth are promised that will never ever pass through the eye of the needle. Be warned and warn those who deliberately market the name of Jesus as a brand and the cross as their logo.

"The good news used as a source of income for some has become bad news for many who don't have a penny. All of man's currencies are of no value in the Kingdom of God and today, many of them are near worthless, and little more than a joke on the earth. What many value on the earth is worthless in God's sight. Currencies have, and will continue to be devalued, so heed the greed [pay attention / take notice of] and take note of the mote in your eye. For I am bringing down My hammer on the earth like an auctioneer, and have set a reserve price on all that pertains to the name of Jesus, so you will no longer be able to do your own bidding. All that is fake and counterfeit will be rejected, and thrown out where there will be weeping and gnashing of teeth.

"Listen I say, listen, I am raising up prophets who will discern that which is false and make it known to you. For many who have eyes to see and ears to hear, do not recognise the sheep from the goats or the wolf in sheep's clothing. In the USA, there is a herb that whips up the flock into a frenzy and believed he could garnish others with a revival anointing at a price, or should I say, at the expense of others. Then there is the special offer, like the green prosperity handkerchief that is not worth blowing your nose in. [C.f. Judges 8:22-27, 2 Kings 18:4, Isaiah 30:2-3, Isaiah 31:1-2, 6 and Isaiah 50:11, objects, situations and circumstances being abused, and God was not pleased!].

"Beware I say, beware of a phoney and his phones, why the rush? Why the hurry? 'Give now!,' they cry. Like the vulture, they will keep coming until all that is left is bone. Yet still they gobble on and on and on like a turkey. Test the spirits I say, test the spirits and read the Bible, testing all that is promised, and claimed with the Word of God. My Spirit comes as a dove and speaks in a small still voice, a whisper.

"Beware, you have been warned."

Michael Backholer, Easter Monday, 25 April 2011 – www.ProphecyNow.co.uk

From Manipulative Media to Divine Grace & to the Oscars (Christian Fundraising by Dishonest Means)

This is what the Sovereign Lord says,

"Against all odds, Saul was anointed King over the Lord's inheritance and My Spirit came upon him in power causing him to prophesy alongside the prophets of his day. Sadly, as so often is the case in the process of time, Saul turned away from Me, ignoring My instructions and I was grieved that I had made him king. In the fullness of time, My Spirit left him and he was tormented by an evil spirit. Later, in desperation he turned to a medium in Endor, who was well versed in witchcraft. From the beginning, Satan has enticed My people to compromise and embrace his way of doing things condoning lies, deceit and deception, luring them to indulge in manipulation, intimidation or domination of others, all of which are at the very heart of witchcraft. I tell you the truth, little has changed.

"Jeremiah warned of those who put their trust in man and depended on flesh for their strength and whose heart turned away from the Lord. Few today truly know the difference between the Spirit of Truth and the spirit of falsehood. There are actors in Hollywood and actors in the Church. I tell you the truth, the Holy Spirit is the Director of all things Divine on the earth today and cannot be stage-managed by any man or woman. No matter how hard you try to deceive yourself and others of His presence, it is in truth a Satanic delusion of a mind that has not been fully transformed. The heart of man is desperately wicked and deceitful above all things.

"For many today, raising money is a mockery of manmade ideas that tries to replace Divine grace with human ability. While doing their best to manipulate and deceive others, they themselves are being manipulated and deceived. Jesus said, "I am sending you out like sheep among wolves, therefore be as shrewd as snakes and as innocent as doves because the people of the world are more shrewd in dealing with their own kind than are the people of the light."

"It is with deepest regret, great sadness and profound sorrow that I say to you, 'If there were nominations for an annual mockery-award for hyperactive individuals, who are well versed and trained in the ancient art of prostituting themselves (while manipulating others for money); more than a few members of the church media circus would win the award.' These wolves in sheep's clothing are highly paid to extract money fraudulently, whilst implying that the Holy Spirit is aiding and abetting them. They would win the award for, the most embarrassing, outlandish, far-fetched, misrepresentation of the truth to raise money in My name.

"There are those who I called and anointed to represent Me in the media, and just as Saul did, they have ignored My instructions and turned to those who masquerade as My servants and who are not. You are all without excuse. I have not forgotten how one who masquerades, bullied My servants into submission while on-air for all to see (to embrace his lies, deceit and deception) and the look of horror on their faces as the conviction of the Holy Spirit took hold of them. I warn you now, take account, as you account, for you surely will be called to give an account for this flagrant abuse of the truth.

"It is lunacy to think that you can embrace demonic ways and amalgamate them with the Divine. It is lunacy to employ devilish ways and means. I ask you, where is the fruit? Witchcraft is an act of the sinful nature. The difference could not be plainer to see, one is like a yellow brick road, the other a road of gold as transparent as glass. Do you see it? Do you wish to? It was a revelation to one media ministry, which is now transparent without walls to hide behind. Listen, while you continue to exploit and manipulate others, you will reap what you have sown. You have become bewitched like the foolish Galatians and are trying to obtain your goal by human effort. You address My people as saints, but are no longer as God-fearing as you once were yourselves. Have you suffered so much behind the screens for nothing? What will it take for you to be still in order that you can hear Me clearly once more? You know from old not to place your faith in gold. Solomon received 666 talents of gold each year and more, but still did evil in My sight (in the eyes of the Lord). Even with all his wealth and wisdom, he too was led astray by others to embrace ways that grieved and displeased Me. No matter how many talents you raise now with your talent without Me, how will you raise it later without the mark 666?

"As for those self-serving satanic servants of manipulation who slither from one ministry to another letting off steam, they are empty kettles and as stiff-necked as the Tin Man without the true oil of anointing."

Michael Backholer, 18 Dec. 2011 – www.ProphecyNow.co.uk

Some Christian meetings and Christian television programmes are overshadowed by emotional or manipulative appeals for money, with secular style fundraising (as distinct from honest appeals, 1 Corinthians 16:1 and 2 Corinthians 11:7-9). These individuals live like millionaire celebrities whilst taking from the poor and needy 'for dishonest gain' (1 Peter 5:2). Many professional 'Christian' fundraisers make unscriptural claims, use high-pressure sales techniques and are guilty of the sin of simony (Acts 8:18-23), by offering Divine blessings / favour for your financial gift or repeated donations, and they want MORE!

Chapter 16

The Great Commission and Warfare

Jesus said, "Go into all the world and preach the gospel to every creature. He who believes and is baptised will be saved; but he who does not believe will be condemned" (Mk. 16:15-16).

Peace Versus the Sword
(Full Surrender for the Great Commission)

This is what the Sovereign Lord says,

"From 2006 onwards, My sword began its journey passing through this nation (UK),[1] the nations of the world, people groups, families and the Church. Jesus made it very plain when He said, 'I did not come to bring peace but a sword, to divide and separate sheep from goats and wheat from tares.' Micah in his day revealed this truth to Israel (Micah 7:5-6). From the beginning the enemy has strived to bring a widespread cross-current fog of deception, of counterfeit thoughts, ideas and man's plans to deceive, distract, delay, deflect, redirect or derail My people. Like those lukewarm Laodiceans who are like phlegm in the throat of the Body of Christ (Revelation 3:14-22). There has always been those who are not truly committed and become the devil's plants to sow seeds of strife and division to fracture or break the Body of Christ.

"To many today, the Church has become a refuge and a hiding place, not the power house it is called to be, instead of binding the strong man and pulling down his strongholds (Ephesians 3:10-11 and Ephesians 6:10-18), for many, they themselves are bound and are being dragged down. Return to your first love before it is too late, for I will shut the gate. I am the true Vine and My Father is the Gardener, abide in Me, remain in Me and bear fruit, you cannot bear fruit by yourself.

"Soldiers of the cross are called to lay down their life for their friends. You are My friends if you do what I command, many I say, many have already made a full surrender but not to the

Holy Spirit, but to the world. Do not be deceived, if you do not remain in Me as a branch in the Vine, you will wither away, by yourself you can do nothing, your works will be tested by the fire of the Holy Spirit. To complete the Every Creature Commission I have called and chosen men and women from many nations, who have, or are, in the process of surrendering their bodies to the Holy Spirit to be used as His temple. Those who dare to stand in their way, His way, My way, Our way, will be pruned back or pruned out. Time is short, the Groom is making ready to come for His Bride. In Elijah's day, I reserved seven thousand and in this hour I have set apart many more who will walk in the power of My Spirit in this end-time outpouring of My Spirit on all flesh."

Michael Backholer, 3 July 2011 – www.ProphecyNow.co.uk

1. See chapter three, the first two prophecies.

Claiming and Reclaiming our Birthright
(Spiritual Warfare and Rules of Engagement)

This is what the Sovereign Lord says,

"Today, this day and everyday, I hear the bleating of My sheep, as in Saul's day. For My people are disobedient just like Jonah, whose disobedience rocked the boat he was in, endangering the lives of others. So it was for Moses, day and night My people moaned and groaned, and were disobedient.
"Today, this day and everyday, many who claim to be My disciples are straining at the oars, because the wind of My Spirit is against them and Jesus is about to pass them by. Like the first disciples, their hearts have become hardened and for many, disobedience is the norm. Most of the Church is still wandering in a wilderness of disobedience and defeat. How many truly worship Me in Spirit and in truth? How many engage daily in some form or other of spiritual warfare? Sadly, many have not even tasted the new wine, and are still in their old wineskins, bobbing about on the water being blown here, there, and everywhere, with every wind of teaching, hoping that Jesus will

come to them and pluck them out of the lake of sin and disobedience.

"Open your eyes, I say, open your eyes, look at the fields! They are ripe for harvest. Make ready for we are about to cross the Jordan once again, into the land I promised you, to do battle and claim the unclaimed ground and reclaim the ground lost. There will be the shedding of blood, and do not be surprised when a tribe or two, or half a tribe have no desire to enter fully in. For there will be people that no matter how unpleasant they seem, My people have to evict. To the religious and self righteous, I say, be warned and repent, for prostitutes and their families will enter in, while you remain in the comfort of your own green pastures. This is a figment of your own imagination where your love for Me is like the morning mist, the dew that melts away with the coming of the sun.

"My prophets and intercessors have battled ahead of you, and know that obedience to My Word and to My Holy Spirit is imperative. For there are rules of engagement that must be adhered to, when binding the strong man and pulling down the strongholds of Jericho that would keep you out. These things can only be learnt in complete obedience to the Holy Spirit, as He leads you into the hidden place, the place of intimacy where He reveals My plan's, and the preparations you must make to claim and reclaim the ground.

"There is no shortage of eyes or ears in the Body of Christ, but most are closed to what I am saying and doing. In the first garden that Adam watched over, the serpent who was crafty and cunning, planted his own seed of lies, deceit and deception, and thorns and thistles took root which became barbs and snares. So it is today in the church garden, where tares, weeds and their seeds have been allowed to take root and flourish like leeches on the body sucking the life blood out of it. Tares, weeds and their seeds (counterfeit disciples) that smother, choke and suffocate the true life out of the Church by shading it from the true light of the Word. [C.f. Matthew 13:24-40].

"The only Spirit that should be in My Church and garden is the Holy Spirit; all others are impostors (counterfeit). First catch your fish then clean them. If you allow bad fish with rotten flesh to remain in the basket with the good fish, will not all become putrid in time? Today, this day and everyday, there are those who claim Me as their Lord and Saviour, yet they fraternise with the enemy of their souls. They fellowship with evil unclean spirits, demons. Cast them out, I say, cast them out in the name of Jesus. You must expel them along with those like Korah, Dathan and Abiram. You must deal with the rabble!

"Day three is upon you, wake up, rise up; you have had all the time in the world to get your supplies ready. Now is the time to cross over the Jordan and take possession, and repossess the land I have given you. 'The highest Heavens belong to the Lord, but the earth He has given to man' (Psalm 115:16)."

Michael Backholer, 7 August 2011 – www.ProphecyNow.co.uk

The Lord's Paratroopers
(Theocratic Intervention – Full of the Holy Spirit)

This is what the Sovereign Lord says,

"In the days of Joshua, he learnt at Rephidim through Moses that is was imperative that holy hands be lifted up to the Lord in intercession, if the battle on the earth was to be won. On entering the Promised Land, Joshua was reminded that he too must look to and listen to the Commander of the Army of the Lord (the captain of the Host), and in doing so victory was assured at Jericho. Sadly, Achan acted unfaithfully towards the Lord and His instructions, which cost the Lord's people dearly in their next battle at Ai.

"Jesus learned obedience through His suffering, as did Paul and all the other apostles. Many today repel discipline and suffering yet willingly embrace denominational denial of biblical truth. Even Barnabas was led astray for a time in his day. The enthusiasm of the flesh knows no bounds, encouraged as it is by the sinful self-nature of the flesh. That which is not crucified under the direction of the Holy Spirit will lead many into self-deception and delusion, believing that they can take or win whole towns, cities and nations without the leading or direction of the Holy Spirit.

"Even now says the Spirit of the Lord there are those who would rather undertake sponsored runs, walks, climbs, swims and all manner of ways to raise money to carry out their own religious plans and ideas, rather than humble themselves, pray and seek My face and turn from their wicked ways. Rather than seek for My Kingdom, My will, My righteousness and see all their needs met in Christ Jesus. I want men everywhere to lift up holy hands in prayer without anger or disputing; clean hands and pure hearts are what I have called for, and will continue to call for. The flesh counts for nothing and needs no motivating, it is the Spirit that counts, poetic rhythm and rhyme sounds good for a season, and may awaken the flesh momentarily but will not revive the spirit of the man or the Church. All of man's own plans, ideas, ambitions, programmes, strategies and agendas have all failed to bring about the completion of My commission – to go into all the world and make disciples, teaching them to obey all I commanded, with signs and miracles following the preaching of My Word. Now is the time to become theocratic (the direct intervention and authority of God working through revelation through man).

"There are those who have had their fill of man's religious and democratic plans and ideas, and are crying out in heartfelt repentance, desperate for the Holy Spirit to enter them and use them for My glory. So, now in the fullness of My time I will release men and women who have been hidden away for such a time as this. Those who have desired more than the baptism of My Spirit (washing over them), but a full and complete surrender of their bodies and wills, so that the Holy Spirit can enter them in all His fullness, power and will, to work in and through them.

"It is written that seven men were chosen who were full of wisdom, faith and the Holy Spirit to wait on tables. Likewise, these hidden ones have humbled themselves in keeping with My will. Soon they will be released and like Philip, miraculous signs shall follow the preaching of My Word, and like Philip and Ezekiel there will be times when they will be taken by the Spirit from one place to another in the twinkling of an eye, from riots to revival. These are the ones that the Holy Spirit fought spiritual battles for, through the consecrated bodies that he had possession of in Swansea,[1] in Wales, in Great Britain (the United Kingdom). At that crossroads in time, they and their nation were all united as one (a transverse section of people fully representative of a nation and God's will). These hidden ones are some of the ones that intercession was undertaken for in the last days. As in the beginning (the day of Pentecost), they will address the crowds with tongues of fire, so that all present will hear and understand them in their own native language, and they too shall be cut to the heart and repent. Then the world will truly stand up and take notice as kings and queens, and all in leadership, good, bad and evil alike will know that Jesus is Lord and will have to choose to repent or perish. The hidden ones shall appear from nowhere, uninvited, no announcements or introductions necessary for their appearing will be suddenly, as the Angel of the Lord appeared out of nowhere. Even in jungles, there are groups of people still hidden and not known, but I know them and I shall visit them in keeping with My Word, through the ones that I have chosen and set apart for such a time as this."

1. This is a reference to Rees and Samuel Rees Howells and the team of intercessors at the former Bible College of Wales who acquiesced with the Person of the Holy Spirit. They took up the challenge to intercede for the completion of the Every Creature Commission; whatever the cost and the cost was unimaginable to the majority of the Body of Christ. The price having been paid in full under the shadow of the cross and washed in the blood of the Lord Jesus Christ.

Michael Backholer, 15 July 2012 – www.ProphecyNow.co.uk

The greatest enemy to each individual is self – self that has not surrendered to God – we have not offered our bodies as 'living sacrifices' which is merely our reasonable service (Romans 12:1), nor taken up our cross daily and followed the Master. All too often it is not Thy will be done, but *my will* be done. The apostle Paul wrote: 'He [Jesus] died for all, that those who live should no longer live for themselves, but for Him who died for them and rose again' (2 Corinthians 5:15). Self must be crucified and dethroned. '...I might live to God. I have been crucified with Christ; it is no longer I who live, but Christ lives in me; and the life which I now live in the flesh I live by faith in the Son of God...' (Galatians 2:19-20). We are not our own as we have been bought at a great price and should glorify God (1 Corinthians 6:19-20). If you confess that Jesus Christ is Lord then you must allow Him to be in *full* control, walking in the Spirit, full of the Spirit and being led of the Spirit.

Chapter 17

Facing Hard Truths – The Church

Thus says the Lord God, "I will make them and the places all around My hill a blessing; and I will cause showers to come down in their season; there will be showers of blessing. Then the trees of the field shall yield their fruit, and the earth shall yield her increase..." (Ezekiel 34:26-27).

Seasons of Healing
(The World will Stand Up and Take Notice)

This is what the Sovereign Lord says,

"Flipping through the calendar of time, you cannot help but notice that there are seasons for every activity under the sun, times to sow and times to grow. Seasons and places of grace and encouragement in this present season, a seed of faith and expectation has germinated, taken root and grows for the long awaited season of healing miracles. Listen, I say, listen, take note and learn from those who went before you. Those who have taken the time and care to read that which others took the time and care to write, to provide for you, so you could know the truth and embrace Him who sets the captives free.

"Every good and perfect gift is from above coming down from the Father. With God all things are possible for those who truly believe, look up, I say, look up! Look back, I say, look back! Jesus is the same yesterday and today and forever. Some were called to look up to a bronze snake to live (Numbers 21). Another was told to go and wash seven times in the Jordan River to be cleansed and restored (2 Kings 5). Others went up on a mountainside to be healed (Matthew 15:29-31). While others followed Jesus for days from one region to another to be healed (Matthew 19:1-2), and some even carried their sick on their beds into the streets in the hope that the shadow of a man passing by might come on them for healing (Acts 5:15). One man was invalid for thirty-eight years, yet walked (John 5).

Consider carefully the part you may have to play if you are to be made whole in this end-time season of outpouring.

"Down the corridors of time you pass the hall of mirrors, some stop and have a hard look at themselves. As water reflects the face, so a man's heart reflects the man. Examine yourselves; open your hearts up to the Word of God and to the Holy Spirit. Allow the sunshine of His love to illuminate the dark recesses of your mind and then deal with all that has taken root in light of God's Word, which is living and active. Sharper than any double-edged sword, it penetrates even to the dividing of soul and spirit, joints and marrow. It judges the thoughts and attitudes of the heart.

"Let those who have ears hear what the Spirit says to the Church, for the days of powerless shadows are coming to an end and the true Church will embrace a season of healing miracles, signs and wonders that will bring glory to God, and the world will sit up, stand up and take notice. But many will reject this outpouring of Grace, yet for those who truly believe and embrace it, it shall be as liquid love, warm and sweet as honey oozing from the Throne Room through the Body of Christ. What you have seen so far is but a trickle in springtime, but as faith rises so shall the Son. As His sun rises so shall the temperature and the honey of His love shall gurgle as a spring of living water flowing into a brook, running into a stream. And streams of living water will flow as a river of life, flowing from the Throne of God and of the Lamb. This is indeed liquid love, like the blood of the Lamb for the healing of the nations."

Michael Backholer, Sunday 19 June 2011, (Father's Day, UK) – www.ProphecyNow.co.uk

The Long Wrong Road to Nineveh
(Your Way or God's?)

This is what the Sovereign Lord says,

"What, O what are My people up to now? What, O what are they doing? Do they know themselves? Many who claim they are My people have a never-ending supply of adrenalin to do what *they* want to do. They continually come up with new ideas on how they can reach their generation. They will travel over land and sea by trains, boats and planes or trundle in cars on roads made from tar, and continue in the wrong direction like Jonah. They make great boasts of what I can do, then continue to do their own thing. Why, O why do you think that only a few truly reach so many? Why, O why do you think that so few walk in the power of My Spirit, and I am not referring to those who rant and rave like those with road rage and claim it as My anointing. Your flesh is never-ending like the roads you travel on.

"The very thing I want the most, is the very same thing you value the most. The very same thing I want from you, you have no wish to part with. You claim to be dead to this world but are in fact more alive than bees in their hive. When it comes to your will, you are as aggressive as a wasp in a fruit tree but lack the fruit yourself. You are more sensitive to your own will and comfort than you are to My Spirit. This is why so many of you spend so much time on the roundabout of self deception, going round in circles but never reaching the destination that I have for you.

"You say you only want My good, pleasing and perfect will. You receive the gifts of My Spirit, but refuse Him the very thing He wants from you, yet claim is His. You say your body is the temple of the Holy Spirit, but is it? My good, pleasing and perfect will is that you surrender your body as a living sacrifice to the Holy Spirit and be transformed by the renewing of your mind. Then and only then will you be able to test and approve what My good, pleasing and perfect will truly is. Can you honestly say you have been crucified with Christ? Can you honestly say you no longer live? Can you honestly say the life that you live in the body, you live by faith in the Son of God who loves you and gave Himself for you?

"What of your character, has the sanctifying work of the Holy Spirit caused you to live a holy life? Just as moths are drawn to the beams of light from a car's headlights, so you are drawn into the light of Christ by the Holy Spirit. But, unlike the moths, as you draw near to the source of the light you are unwilling to lay down your will or your life for His. Again and again, you swerve back and forth into the darkness and follow your own sinful Sat-Nav of self-will and bright ideas, that like a candle burns out. You talk of the baptism of My Spirit as if it were a set of new tyres to aid you on your journey, as you race from one place to another. Pull over, I say, pull over, apply the brakes, you are heading towards a precipice, the end of the road. Repent, turn around and like Jonah, go in the direction I have called you.

"If as you claim your body is the temple of the Holy Spirit and He lives in you and you abide in Him, then He teaches you all things and reminds you of everything that I have said. Then pray tell Me, why, O why do you go here, there and everywhere in search of Him, His power and to be in His presence? Could it be that your old sinful nature (your flesh) has still not been crucified with Christ and you are still very much alive to this world, that you claim only to be passing through and not a part of? While you are still on the road of self-will, others I have called, you to are being overlooked or lost. You will recall Jonah was thrown into the sea of God's mercy and compassion and was swallowed by a great fish. Like the prodigal son, he came to his senses and recalled that those who cling to worthless idols forfeit the grace that could be theirs. There are billions upon billions today like those in Nineveh, who cannot tell their right hand from their left, and I am equally concerned for them. But you appear not to be, as you continue to head for Tarshish and on down the road to Joppa. Be warned, a great wind and a violent storm is on the way for many, but you must choose your will, your way or Mine? For many will be washed up on a beach like trash."

Michael Backholer, 13 Nov. 2011 – www.ProphecyNow.co.uk

31·1·2017

Full and unconditional surrender to the will of God (Romans 12:1) is putting to death the old man and exchanging your life for His; a giving of yourself to be *entirely* at His disposal and to hate the things of the world so that they have no hold over you (1 John 2:15-17). Your dreams, ambitions, desires, your money, your nearest and dearest, your will, your very self and all that is you, is laid upon God's altar. As you die to self, the more you surrender (every area of self and sin), the more you can be filled with the Holy Spirit, who is given without measure. Then you can live entirely for the glory of God and to be led of the Holy Spirit, exalting Jesus Christ because there is none of you (John 3:30), but the Spirit of God in you.

Tuesday night in bed will cont 9.28pm.

Chapter 18

Tares, Hirelings and Pruning

"...Woe to the shepherds of Israel who feed themselves! Should not the shepherds feed the flocks? You eat the fat and clothe yourselves with wool; you slaughter the fatlings, but you do not feed the flock" (Ezekiel 34:2b-3).

While the People Slept
(The Enemy Sowed Tares – Spiritual Terrorists)

This is what the Sovereign Lord says,

"Now is the time for every fellowship, every assembly that is part of My Body to be vigilant. While My people slept the enemy sowed tares / weeds in your midst, some of which have been there for a long time and are deep rooted and difficult to see because they have concealed themselves. They are strategically placed spiritual terrorists. Do not say, 'Surely this does not include us?' for it may. Now is not the time to bury your heads in the sand or turn a blind eye, but it is imperative that all exercise wisdom and discernment. This is what will happen before that great and glorious day which I have planned and purposed – when I shall pour out My Spirit all over Great Britain (like never before witnessed in these islands).

"I have warned you of wolves in sheep's clothing, I said, 'You shall know them by their fruit.' Be warned, many are hiding behind good works, but do not be fooled by outward appearances. This calls for cool heads and sound minds, for when My Spirit begins to move in real power, you could be caught off guard and taken by surprise at the level of opposition by some; to this end-time move of My Spirit." [See Matthew 7:15-20 and Matthew 10:16].

Michael Backholer, 17 April 2007 – www.ProphecyNow.co.uk

"Woe to the shepherds who destroy and scatter the sheep of My pasture!" says the Lord (Jeremiah 23:1). C.f. Zech. 11:17.

Hired Hands Care Little for the Sheep
(Prayer and Bible Study are Neglected)

This is what the Sovereign Lord says,

"In its day! The Gardens of Helegan, (Cornwall, UK), produced the finest vegetables and most succulent of fruits to grace the table of any man and his family. Unfortunately, with the coming of war (World War I), the peace and tranquillity was lost, along with much of its workforce and so it came to pass that the estate and gardens slipped slowly but surely into disrepair with decades of neglect. Once again, thorns and thistles returned in abundance, and the ivy and brambles of time knitted together as a shroud, and it was veiled from the sight of man. But in the fullness of time it was rediscovered quite by chance or so the world has been led to believe.

"But I AM Sovereign and in control of all things and all things are under My control. Therefore, I am able to work in and through any man or woman that I choose to, to bring about My purposes on the earth. Yes, I say, yes, there are times when I choose to work through the most unlikely of people in the most unlikely of ways. This garden is an analogy of parts of the Church where prayer and Bible study are very much neglected, or forgotten altogether, and the true unity of being one in spirit is little understood. In its place, the spirit of division rules the day, as individuals born of the flesh, but not born of the Spirit, war against each other for selfish gain.

"Do not be deceived, you will reap what you sow, woe to those shepherds who only take care of themselves and not the flock. The weak are not strengthened, those who are sick, bound and injured are left to themselves while the strays still stray, and those who are lost are forgotten. Many have ruled harshly and brutally, and have scattered to the hills and homes.

"Hear the word of the Lord this day, hear, I say, listen to the Spirit of the living God. I will hold to account every shepherd who puts himself first and remove those who do not repent and turn I say, turn from their wicked ways. Many have grown fat off the land, and off the lambs, and off the backs of others and yet feel no shame. Sheep without a shepherd wander off in all directions and many are devoured by dead denominations that once lived. While others are caught and ensnared by the brambles of despair, while still others drop with exhaustion and dehydration for lack of feeding and drinking on the living Word. In this hour when hearts are weighed down by the weight of the ivy of time, and neglect that has choked out the true light of the Word, and the Bread of Heaven lays hidden beneath the continual propagation of the weeds of doom and gloom.

"I have this to say, My Spirit will shepherd My flock, My sheep know My voice and together we shall reclaim the ground lost or neglected [Ezekiel 34:11 and 1 Peter 2:25]. My Spirit will plough and re-plough, and there shall be a harvest, a great harvest and My Spirit shall shepherd in this great harvest as He is poured out from on high. Wake up, get up, read up, pray up, feed up, and look up. If you would understand My meaning, I am removing the shrink-wrap and de-waxing My combine harvesters in readiness. So make ready, sharpen your scythes, sickles and hooks. Repair your rakes to glean and gather in the remnants of the harvest alongside My combines.

"Be on your guard; be alert, for as My combine harvesters combine with the true Church harvesters to gather in the harvest. The vermin, tares, weeds and their seed along with the mockers and the troublemakers, who have hidden away under a canopy of religious confusion, will scurry out into the open to do all they can to hinder, discourage and slow down My chosen ones for they know their end, and their end is near."

Michael Backholer, 11 Sept. 2011 – www.ProphecyNow.co.uk

Tares and Wood-Wormed Chairs
(Spring-Clean – Infested, Fumigated or Demolished)

This is what the Sovereign Lord says,

"In My house there are many rooms that are full of the light of the world and spotless. But this is not the case in the house of God which is made up of many rooms, many of which are full of darkness and the things of this world that moth and rust will destroy. Some have been broken into by thieves and they have stolen the true treasure of the heart of the Church. So great is the darkness that has overcome some of the rooms that should have been filled with the light of My overcomers, that now, the spirit of Islam abides as a testimony against those who claimed to be My disciples. They did not walk in the light as He is in the light, so that the blood of Jesus would purify them from ALL sin.

"Many I say, many have spent their time digging holes like chambers down a mineshaft to meet and greet each other so that their own minds have chasms of the abyss of darkness. Caves for slaves of sin where the darkness is so dense that their eyes have become allergic to the truth of the true light.

"You know all about the Arab Spring as presented by the media, but neglect the Scriptures that foretold the events. I AM Sovereign and in control of all things, and all things are under My control. I know all that has happened, is happening and will happen, for I AM the Alpha and the Omega, yet you have failed to notice My spring-clean. Yes, I say, yes, My Spirit is spring-cleaning the rooms of My house, the house of God, the Church, the Body of Christ and where it meets. I AM pulling out the furniture that many have hidden behind to reveal, and get at, the dirt hidden by the darkness of generations of religious dust and musty cobwebs, where flies and lies have been cocooned by the spiders of deceit and deception. The hidden places where serpents and scorpions have had the freedom to wander and bite without fear of being crushed under heel. [See Nehemiah 4:7-8, Nehemiah 6:1-2 and Nehemiah 13:7-9].

"I am pulling down the blinds that have blinded so many to the full truth of the gospel, and I am burning the furniture that is riddled with worm and beetle, not forgetting the lice and mice that have infested the echelons of manmade denominations. If the owner of the house had kept watch as instructed, the thief who comes to steal, kill, and destroy would not have entered by invitation.

"Just as My house has many rooms so My Vine has many branches and all have to be tended. Houses that are infested must be fumigated and some demolished. Diseased or dead branches in the Vine are pruned out and thrown onto the fire, listen, I say, listen. I say again, and again, and again, listen to the Word of the Lord. The Holy Spirit will illuminate tares, weeds, and their seed in the house of God. I will cause a vacuum to suck the muck into the light for all to see who wish to. My house will be called a house of prayer for all nations, not a den of God robbers as many have made it. Consider carefully what I have said this day and meditate upon it for as it is written so it shall be done. To those who need to repent, I say repent now, while there is still time."

Michael Backholer, 7 August 2011 – www.ProphecyNow.co.uk

'In the last days perilous times will come, for men will be lovers of themselves, lovers of money.... Lovers of pleasure rather than lovers of God, having a form of godliness but denying its power. And from such people turn away! ...But evil men and impostors will grow worse and worse, deceiving and be deceived' (2 Timothy 3:1-2, 4, 13).

Sitting on the Fence of Defence
(Facing Truths – Tares and Sons of the Evil One)

This is what the Sovereign Lord says,

"For generations My chosen ones have sat on a fence on the defence because the name of Jesus is an offence to many. Now is the time to come down off this fence that you have been nailed to, and rise up in resurrection power in the name of Jesus, and the blood of the Lamb to claim the very ground that you stand on. You have suffered what you have tolerated; in almost every fellowship there are those who do not have in mind the things of God, but the things of men. They are stumbling blocks to the name of Jesus and the good news of the gospel. [Phil. 1:15, Titus 1:11, 1 John 2:19 and 3 John 10].

"Many I say, many are being mocked by the few, but I will not be mocked; in every fellowship those who sow to please their sinful nature shall surely reap destruction. To the many parts of the Body of Christ, I have this to say – it is not a climb down, but a step up when you face and deal with those tares who are the sons of the evil one sown by the devil. If My chosen ones had spent as much time in My Word, in prayer and in My presence as they have sat on the fence, then their eyes would have been opened to the truth.

"I AM pulling down this fence of indecision and you will be compelled to face the truth that has been staring you in the face for generations. But My people have been unwilling to face it or deal with it. I have given My Church all the power they need to stand in victory against the enemy, but you must use it as I direct. I know of the frustration and anger that some of you feel, knowing that some in leadership do not have in mind the things of God, but their own selfish will. In all things I would encourage you to look to Me in prayer and in My Word, and allow the Holy Spirit the responsibility of leading you in the outworking of every situation. Your struggle is not with flesh and blood. You must stand against the enemy in the full armour of God. Be strong in Me, and My mighty power to come against the devil's schemes.

"Listen I say, listen to the Spirit of the Lord, you are in the final hour of the last day and will be compelled to choose. The choice is yours and yours alone, no servant can serve two masters. If you are wedded to the world, you cannot love or be devoted to Me. For there are those in the Church this day that despise Me, My true teachings and those who are devoted to Me. Again I say, this is the last hour and in this hour you are called to test all things against the Word of God. You have also been called to test the spirits, for you do not recognise the difference between the Spirit of Truth and the spirit of falsehood. How then will you recognise the spirit of the antichrist that is already in the world?

"Bad company corrupts good character; diseased branches spread disease, yeast ferments through the whole batch of the dough. Polluted people desecrate, violate, and profane that which is sacred and in time convert it to evil use. Even now, as the Spirit of God speaks, many of you are still confused and in your hearts are saying, 'What has this to do with me?' Listen, these people honour Me with their lips, but their hearts are far from Me. Why are you so dull? It is the righteous who will shine like the sun in their Father's Kingdom. The tares, the weeds are goats who do not hear or wish to hear the Shepherd's voice. They are wolves in sheep's clothing and are ferocious, and come to scatter the flock, to divide, separate and lead astray to devour. These cunning old wolves have made their lair in the sheep pen and will not rest day or night. You must drive them out. At the end of the age, the Son of Man will send out His angels, and they will weed out of His Kingdom everything that causes sin and all who do evil. He who has ears let him hear."

Michael Backholer, 4 Sept. 2011 – www.ProphecyNow.co.uk

An enemy can be a secret informer (Nehemiah 6:10) or false brethren who have come to spy (Galatians 2:4-5). 'For certain men have crept in unnoticed, who long ago were marked out for this condemnation, ungodly men who turn the grace of our God into licentiousness and deny the only Lord God and our Lord Jesus Christ' (Jude 4). Enemies can sit in silent opposition with smiles on their faces but with anger and bitterness in their hearts. An enemy can also be a tare, a plant from the devil who has infiltrated your church, Bible College / Seminary or ministry. Tobiah hated the Jews yet wormed his way into the temple of the Lord and even set up his home! (Nehemiah 13:4-9). Some tares having been taken captive to do the devil's will (2 Timothy 2:26 and 2 Timothy 3:6) can be set free (delivered from demons), whilst others can only be distinguished and separated at the end of the age (Matthew 13:26-40). Tares can be so deceived and deluded that they really believe that God is with them, yet they are fighting against Him, by opposing His servants, 'deceiving and be deceived' (2 Timothy 3:13). They can also be wolves in sheep's clothing (Matthew 7:15).

The Church Coppice
(Lessons from Nature, Tares, Youth and Social Networks)

This is what the Sovereign Lord says,

"In My coppice of ash, hazel, and oak you will find a cradle of youth that reach up to the light, sturdy and resolute. The old growth is pruned out and used in all manner of ways, but some are burned to charcoal. With the light pouring in through the canopy, the woodland floor comes alive in season with a blaze of primroses, violets, cowslips, bluebells and wild daffodils. As they push through the carpet of moss, lichen and leaves, all manner of birds and animals grace this place of extreme life and activity. Some are nocturnal, preferring the darkness to the light, when they are most active along with the weeds and their never-ending supply of seeds. But, in this place of natural beauty something sinister is taking place. ["What do you see?" Jeremiah 1:11, Ezekiel 8:12, Amos 7:8 and Zechariah 4:2].
"Flashes of colour like Joseph's coat can be seen as kingfishers dart and dive into the streams, while jays and

pheasants call out to the drumbeat of the woodpecker. But, there is another sound that is quite unique and a warning to all, that danger lurks in the undergrowth. The migratory cuckoo has returned to lay her eggs in another's nest, just like the devil plants his tares in the Church. The cuckoo is full of lies, deceit and deception and will lay it's eggs in the nests of others, and even though her eggs are not identical as the hosts, they are more often than not indistinguishable from the others. But, in the fullness of time the chicks hatch out and begin to push out the hosts chicks and eggs from their nest, just like the thief who comes to steal, kill and destroy. Hidden by the mist of deception and the daily dawn chorus, the cuckoo goes about her wicked work while the other bird's backs are turned.

"This is also the case with the cradle of youth, the young with all the vigour of youth jumping and bouncing up and down, hands raised, with loud cries and shouts as if they were on fire for the Lord. Yes, they proclaim we are the generation that the Lord will use. Yes, says the Lord, I shall indeed use some, but as in Gideon's day, I will sift the many and remove them that lap like dogs and choose the ones that kneel before Me. Those who lap like dogs, bark like dogs – like charcoal – they turn up at every Bar-B-Q and howl for all to hear, but so do wolves in sheep's clothing. Many a tongue is a liar who claims to be on fire, but those with sore knees hidden by trees are the ones I shall transform into mighty warriors and place true tongues of fire on them. [C.f. Acts 1:4-8, Acts 2:1-4 with James 3:6-8].

"The tongue makes great boasts, it is also a fire, a world of evil among the Body of Christ that can and will corrupt the whole person, and draw them towards the fires of Hell. So be warned young ones, you may yet be bagged by the poacher and like charcoal finish up on the shelf in Tesco or Wal-Mart. Young ones, I am calling you like I called Zacchaeus, come down off your pedestal, today I must stay at your house. 'Wicked,' you say, 'wicked,' what manner of spirit speaks from your mouth? Think next before you text, why twitter with a heart that is bitter and head full of litter? Do you truly want Me in your house oh little church mouse? What might I find that you leave behind? When visiting the house of God, have a long look, friend of Facebook for My friends do what I command; do you?"

Michael Backholer, 2 October 2011 – www.ProphecyNow.co.uk

Chapter 19

Asia – Korea and Japan

'The Lord takes pleasure in those who fear Him, in those who hope in His mercy.... He sends out His commands to the earth; His word runs very swiftly. He gives snow like wool; and scatters the frost like ashes; He casts His hail like morsels; who can stand before His cold? He sends His word and melts them; He causes His wind to blow, and the waters flow.... Praise the Lord!' (Psalm 147:11, 15-18, 20b).

Korea – One Nation
(The Unification of North and South)

This is what the Sovereign Lord says,

"Jesus Christ of Nazareth will be lifted up on high over North Korea, and a new day shall dawn, says the Spirit of the Lord. To the eye of man, the flames and fire of Pyongyang were extinguished under an avalanche of lies, deceit and deception, smothering the glow of life, out of the hearts and minds of My people.[1] Behold I say, behold (watch and see), as the fire of the Holy Spirit comes again and melts the fog of deception, then unbelief and denial shall be banished (condemned to exile). Then the bellows of the Lord will bring forth new life. The fire and the flames of revival will leap for joy into the darkness, and My people will bellow out the good news.

"Yes I say, yes, there will be a marriage made in Heaven (God's will). 'No, no, no,' they cry out, 'this cannot happen,' but the Spirit of the Lord says, 'With God nothing is impossible,' look at Germany. If I choose to betroth one to another that is My choice, My will. Furthermore, when My people lift their shields of faith as one, all the flaming arrows of the evil one shall be extinguished in the name of Jesus; the name that is above all other names."

Michael Backholer, Pentecost Sunday, 27 May 2012 – www.ProphecyNow.co.uk

1. In September 1866, Rev. Robert Jermain Thomas soaked Korea with his blood, and became known as the first Protestant missionary and martyr to Korea when he was stabbed, beaten and finally beheaded at Pyongyang (the present capital of North Korea). The Korean Church was founded in 1885, and in 1886, the first Korean was baptised. The Pyongyang Great Revival (1907-1910), saw 50,000 converts in its first year. By 1910, there were 250,000 Christians worshipping God in more than 2,000 churches. After the Korean War (1950-1953), though there had been fighting since 1946, Korea was partitioned at the 38th parallel. Communists ran the North, and North Korea declined in prosperity and freedom, whilst South Korea was democratic, and prospered economically and spiritually.

Japan's Church – Land of the Rising Sun
(Your Hour of Growth)

This is what the Sovereign Lord says,

"To the Church in the garden of Japan, land of the rising sun, I am the true Gardener and My Son is the true Vine. You have known much pruning, but now is the time for new shoots to sprout and form branches that will bear abundant fruit, fruit that will last, fruit that will be turned into new wine.

"Look at the fig tree and all the trees in My garden; when they sprout leaves you know that summer is near. Like the fig tree planted in the vineyard with nothing to show, the Gardener never gave up but dug around it and fertilised it (Luke 13:6-9). So, I say unto you, this will be your hour of growth, as My Son rises far above you and reigns, so shall the sunshine of My love rain down upon you. Many have called you Bonsai, but I have called you to grow as the mustard seed grows, and to form branches like the vine that are far-reaching, producing a vintage that I am proud of and most palatable."

Michael Backholer, 10 June 2012 – www.ProphecyNow.co.uk

'So they shall fear the name of the Lord from the west, and His glory from the rising sun; when the enemy comes in like a flood the Spirit of the Lord will lift up a standard against him' (Isaiah 59:19).

Chapter 20

Tares, Deception and Grace

Jesus said, "If you love Me, keep My commandments and I will pray the Father, and He will give you another Helper, that He may abide with you forever, even the Spirit of Truth, whom the world cannot receive, because it neither sees Him nor knows Him; but you know Him, for He dwells with you and will be in you" (John 14:15-17).

One in Spirit and in Truth
(Divine or Devilish, the Holy Spirit or Tares and Apostasy)

This is what the Sovereign Lord says,

"The Spirit gives life, the flesh counts for nothing (John 6:63). The arm of the flesh is long and far-reaching, and if not crucified, can, and will make a reproduction of the true Church. Satan and his demonic hordes are always on the lookout for those they can work through to counterfeit the real thing. Many are ordained of men to do the work of God, but what is required in this hour is men and women ordained of God to do His will.

"If the Bride is not truly besotted by the Groom, it is only a matter of time before she could become bewitched by another. In every generation, there are those who have Divine appointments with the Holy Spirit, only later to be deceived by a devilish appointment and another spirit, which lures them away from the truth. They become confused and can become willing receptacles of the deceiver, the father of lies. Instead of becoming one in spirit and in truth with the Holy Spirit, they become of two minds, two opinions, double-minded and unstable in all they do.

"The Body of Christ (the Church) is made up of individuals who should all be of one Spirit and one Truth. There should be unity of the Spirit in the bond of peace; one Body, one Spirit, one hope, one Lord, one faith, one baptism, one God and Father of all. Different gifts, but one Spirit, different kinds of service, but one Lord, different ministries, but one God.

"If you abide in Me, you shall remain a part of the Vine; those who choose not to abide cannot remain. If you do not abide or remain, you will not be able to discern My voice. If you are not truly a part of the Vine, you will be like a branch that is thrown away, outside My hedge of protection. Those who say they are My friends yet refuse to do what I command are deceived. If you are unwilling to love others as I have loved you, then you remain a servant, not a friend and cannot know My business.

"Those who are half-hearted will be thrown into the fire, but those who remain and are pruned become clean and fruitful. As they continue to abide in Me they shall be ignited, set ablaze by My Spirit and on fire for Me and My glory. When My Church is truly on fire, the world will turn up to see it burn. As the breath of My Spirit blows on the glowing embers, so shall tongues of fire come upon others, who in turn will become firebrands who will awaken those who are asleep without hope. If the body of man is dead without his spirit then it follows that a church without My Spirit is also dead. Consider these things carefully in light of My Word, for apostasy has taken root in the Church, be warned repent or perish."

Michael Backholer, 10 Jan. 2013 – www.ProphecyNow.co.uk

The End-Time Storms
(Treasures of Heaven or Treasures in Jars of Clay)

This is what the Sovereign Lord says,

"As the mist of time clears along with Satan's fog of deception, those who have chosen to truly focus upon My Word will be able to see in the Spirit more clearly, and be more able and willing to see what the Holy Spirit shows them. For generations, many have seen what they wanted to see and believed what they wanted to believe and are comfortable with.

"It was always My intent and purpose that through the Church, My manifold wisdom would be made plain to the rulers and authorities, the powers of darkness, spiritual forces of evil in the Heavenly realms. Yet, I see before Me a Church (the Body of Christ) meeting inside buildings where all kinds of earthly treasure is stored, where moth, rust, and thieves have all taken their toll. Much of what remains is detestable in My sight, but is greatly valued by some and worshipped by others. There was real concern by some for the buildings and their fittings, but little concern for My name or the treasure of Heaven, the treasure in jars of clay. Are they not of greater value than the carved images of wood or the idols of gold, silver, bronze and stone?

"If My Spirit truly lives in you (are you not the temples of the Holy Spirit?), living stones to be built into a spiritual house; a holy house, a holy priesthood bringing spiritual sacrifices that are acceptable to God through Jesus Christ. I gave strict instructions to Moses on how to build a sanctuary for Me, to dwell among My people. I gave Moses the exact pattern to follow, likewise, Jesus gave the exact instructions on how His Church should be built, led by the Holy Spirit built on the living stone, rejected by man but precious to God. I tell you plainly, if the Lord does not build His house then you labour in vain. Many call Me, 'Lord, Lord,' yet continue to put their own will before Mine, like the man who built his house in My name, he builds on sand, he hears My words but refuses to put them into practice.

"Wake up, wake up, there is a shake up on the way! Wake up from your slumber and the sin of self-sufficiency and admit your poverty. Have you not seen the signs of the end of the age all around you? The beginning of the birth pains. Be not deceived only the unwise and fools refuse to build on the solid rock, the Rock of Ages, a sure and sound foundation that cannot be shaken or washed away. As the level of sin and self-satisfaction continues to rise, so shall the floods and the force of the wind. This is a global warning, a sign that the wind of change, the breath of God, the true power of the Holy Spirit is coming on the Church to prepare her to receive the end-time harvest and make a stand. For another storm will surely follow in time that will crash up against the true and the false houses. One will appear to stand for a time, but being counterfeit, the foundation will be washed away and the house of religion built by man will fall. The other will take a great battering on all sides but will stand firm to the end, as it hangs on to the rock of its salvation.

"The fulfilment of the ages is here and knocking on your door. Man and his plans will wither while the Word of the Lord stands forever. You will be compelled to come into the light, as I AM in the light to see and face the truth. Many I say, far too many are living on borrowed time, the hour of trial is coming. The time of man's assorted association with good and evil will come to a close, and without true faith your hope will diminish. For this shall indeed be a time of great uncertainty when My house, My temples, the temples of the Holy Spirit will be the only ones left standing. Be warned, there is only one foundation that has already been laid; any other foundation is sand, counterfeit and of Satan, and will be washed away. So repent and turn away from sin and all that is selfish; sin and selfishness started with Satan and comes to an end with Satan's end.

Michael Backholer, 1 March 2013 – www.ProphecyNow.co.uk

An Overdraft of Grace Still Outstanding
(What is the True Measure of a Man?)

This is what the Sovereign Lord says,

"Who's fooling who? Do not be deceived, you do indeed reap what you sow. The one who sows to please the Holy Spirit will indeed reap eternal life. But many are reaping a harvest that has come from pleasing their sinful nature, which leads to destruction. They despise being fools for Christ, but willingly embrace being fools in the eyes of the world. They have become bewitched like the Galatians of old, who like them, started with the Spirit and later turned their backs on Him, to put their faith in human effort.

"What is the true measure of a man? How do you measure him? By the size of his ministry, his gifts? Jesus warned that not everyone who says, 'Lord, Lord,' will enter the Kingdom of Heaven, but only those who do the will of His Father in Heaven. Man can and does boast of their deeds of casting out demons, performing miracles and prophesying in My name, only later to be told they are evildoers, that I never knew. The true measure of a man must be measured by the fruit of My Spirit in him. The more fruit he has, the more he is being transformed into the image of Jesus, and will love the Lord his God with all his heart, soul, strength and mind. The measure with which he hates sin is the true measure of His love for Me and My will.

"Ministry can break a man, but it never makes the man something he is not. What truly makes a man, and sets him apart from sin and the world is his relationship with God the Father, through His Son, the Lord Jesus Christ, by the Holy Spirit. Listen, when a man is born again, he opens an account and receives the Holy Spirit as a deposit, who begins to clean out the old vault to make room for something more valuable. The old sinful self-will must be removed and replaced by the greatest treasure a man can receive; God's good, pleasing and perfect will.

"When a man and a woman truly love each other, they get married and enter into a true covenant agreement. They become one, each bringing into the marriage all that they have into a joint account, one in heart and mind, neither claiming any of their possessions as their own, just like the early Church (Acts 4). The Church (the Bride) is covenanted in marriage with Jesus Christ as the Head and the Groom, a joint account made in Heaven. Yet today, many have rejected this and insist on having their own account, their own way, both selfish and independent so they can do as they please, not being accountable to another. They are blind wretched fools, with an overdraft of grace still outstanding, overdrawn and bankrupt of Spirit and truth.

"I have given the Church all it needs in Me to stand in victory against its enemy, but it must use it as the Holy Spirit leads and directs. If an army marches on its stomach, then it follows that before going into war the troops must be trained in warfare, know its enemy and be well fed. This being the case, the true Christian soldier will have on the full armour of God and will feed on the Word of God. So why is it that so few teach the true message of the gospel – the cross, the blood, holiness, sacrifice, Heaven and Hell? What kind of gospel is it that never mentions the work of the Holy Spirit, angels, Satan, evil and unclean spirits? Why the silence on discipleship, Bible study, prayer and intercession?

"Joshua meditated on the Word of the Lord day and night and was instructed to do everything written in it to succeed before going into battle in the Promised Land. Jesus' last words to His disciples was, 'Go and make disciples, teaching them to obey everything I have commanded you.' You claim to be My disciples yet you have not given up everything (Luke 14:33), and what have you done with your gifts, talents and tithes?

Have you invested them or have you built bigger barns to store them in?

"If all you have in your account is the deposit I gave you, you surely will be called to give an account. You cannot bank on what you believe, but only on that which is written in My Word. I have an interest in how you invest all that I have given you. Is it for self or for My Kingdom? While you act like a goat, I have sheep who are starving for bread and a Bible. It is written: 'Man does not live on bread alone, but on every Word that comes from the mouth of God.' You claim to be a child of God, but do little or nothing to help the brothers and sisters in Christ who are malnourished. The only person you are fooling is yourself; as water reflects your face, so your heart reflects who you really are. The fear of the Lord is the beginning of knowledge, but fools despise wisdom and discipline. Woe to the stubborn and self-willed, those who continue in their plans in a coalition, but not with My Spirit, heaping sin upon sin to their everlasting shame."

Michael Backholer, 12 March 2013 – www.ProphecyNow.co.uk

The Church Under Attack: False Teaching, Another Gospel (Living for God, the Great Commission or Man's Mission?)

This is what the Sovereign Lord says,

"The Church will continue to come under increasing pressure as it is infiltrated by tares and swamped by lying, deceiving spirits, antichrist spirits, hell-bent on flooding the Church with lies, deceit and deception. False teaching wrapped up in sweet tasting honey that when swallowed turns sour; it looks good, tastes good, but having been taken in, becomes acrid to the soul. It is bittersweet; the taste of deception that demons drip-feed those who refuse to embrace the truth of God's Word and the Holy Spirit.

"The greatest threat to the Church is Satan's fishers of men who are drip-feeding the lies of 'another gospel' like droplets of honey, slowly sliding down their fishing lines. On reaching the hook, it slowly but surely builds up and glistens until it looks like a fine pearl of gold. This is the bait of Satan and once taken in, the hook is set, and slowly but surely the line is reeled in, until finally, you are ensnared and imprisoned in his net of deception.

"It is a logical progression that can be seen in the most simplest of terms in the parables of Jesus. The parables of the sower, the tares, the fine pearls and the net (Matthew 13). Jesus prophesised about deception in the last days, of wars and rumours of wars, and daily the media reports on them, while the Church is unmoved, and acts as if it has nothing to do with them. So many are content to suck milk through the teat of a baby feeding bottle, but are unwilling to go onto solid food. They are being destroyed from lack of knowledge. They have little or no desire to become Christian soldiers marching as to war, to do battle and see victories like the great awakenings.

"Do not forget there is a way that seems right to a man, but in the end it leads to death. The harvest is indeed still plentiful and still the workers are few. The numbers in Hell increase every second of the day and night, and the angels of the Lord are bemused why the Church does not cry out to the Lord of the harvest to send out more workers. Since the days of John the Baptist, the Kingdom of Heaven has been forcefully advancing and forceful men lay hold of it.

"Jesus rebuked the eleven (Mark 16:14-15) while they were still eating, for their lack of faith and stubborn refusal to believe those He had met and spoken to, after His resurrection. He told them firmly to 'go into all the world and preach the good news to all creation,' and when they went, He worked with them, and through them, and confirmed His Word with signs and wonders. You could be forgiven for asking, what happened to the Decade of Evangelism? Very little, it would appear, and why you ask? Because it was another of man's ideas, born of the flesh not of the Holy Spirit. What of Lakeland you ask? Lakeland was of My Spirit but failed because of the flesh (man's sinful nature), and what of other revivals you ask? The Lord inhabits the praises of His people, when they stop praising, they return to the flesh and only sing about Me. This is not worship, worship is a lifestyle; without holiness no one will see the Lord. So, when the Holy Spirit is grieved He departs.

"Jesus died so that you might live, and yet few are willing to die to self or sin. Few are willing to cry out to the Lord of the harvest. Open your eyes and look at the fields, they are ripe for harvest. Why do you not see the connection, some cry out, others go out, and still others come in. The last day generations with all its wealth and technology will be remembered for how little it did with so much at its disposal. You claim to be a blessed people, yes a people blessed of God. What an honour and a privilege you have – you can help the poor, the underprivileged and the lost whenever you choose to do so. You are truly a most privileged generation, who if you choose, can sit in a lazboy, in the comfort of your own home and watch others on your widescreen televisions, laptops, or on all manner of electronic / digital devices anytime – as millions are forced against their will to become refugees, while others are persecuted for their faith, often beaten to death or starved, while you plan your holidays, vacations and short breaks. You have become lovers of self, lovers of pleasure, lovers of money, not lovers of God.

"You have been warned of terrible times coming in the last days, when the love of most grows cold. You cannot serve God and money, you cannot serve two masters, you will either hate one or love the other. When you hear this, your flesh cries out. Are you trying to make us feel guilty? No, YOU ARE GUILTY; your actions speak louder than your words. Faith without deeds is useless, dead; you believe in God, so do the demons and they shake and shudder! Repent while there is still time. Have you forgotten that when persecution came to the early Church, they were scattered and those who were scattered preached the gospel everywhere they went. So what are you waiting for? Jesus will not return until the good news of the gospel is preached to every nation, tribe, language and people."

Michael Backholer, 18 March 2013 – www.ProphecyNow.co.uk

Oswald J. Smith wrote: 'No sooner have I dealt with sin than I am compelled to deal with self. And so must you. God insists on having first place. Where then do you stand in relation to His will? Have you really surrendered all to Jesus Christ? Do you recognise Him alone as your Lord and Master? Are you willing to go, where He wants you to go, to do what He wants you to do, and to be what He wants you to be? Have you still a will of your own, or is God's will yours, and is it your supreme delight to please Him? Are you sold out to Jesus Christ?

Chapter 21

Spiritual Warfare

'Finally my brethren, be strong in the Lord and in the power of His might. Put on the whole armour of God, that you may be able to stand against the wiles [schemings] of the devil. For we do not wrestle against flesh and blood, but against principalities, against powers, against the rulers of the darkness of this age, against spiritual hosts of wickedness in the Heavenly places' (Ephesians 6:10-12).

War on Two Fronts, Full Surrender for Victory (Spiritual Warfare and the Every Creature Commission)

This is what the Sovereign Lord says,

"Do you need reminding that you are in a war between good and evil, and every battle, every conflict on the earth coincides with spiritual warfare in the Heavenly realms? Both are spiritual in origin, as spiritual forces of evil battle against the Kingdom of God. For the Kingdom of God to prevail on earth as in Heaven, the Church must bind the strong man and pull down his strongholds that coincide over the earth – the rulers of darkness, spiritual hosts of wickedness. It is imperative for every true believer, born of the Spirit, to understand that the conflicts on the earth start in the Heavenly realms and are spiritual in nature, as principalities and powers of darkness battle against angelic forces. It is crucial that the Body of Christ understands it is God's army on the earth, and will be called to make a stand against the antichrist, the man of lawlessness (2 Thessalonians 2).

"In a previous generation, a group of believers were called by the Holy Spirit to surrender all and lay down their lives to intercede, to stop Hitler and his Nazi regime, who wished to set up their own millennial reign on the earth. Before and throughout the Second World War and beyond, often the Body of Christ (the Church), which the Lord God called and planted in the cleft of the rock in Wales, UK, were called into intercession as one in spirit and in truth, as each in turn surrendered to the Holy Spirit. Then as one body, led by the Holy Spirit they fought as one in the end-time battle in the Heavenly realms, at the same time as the military battled on the earth. They were taught by the Holy Spirit that victory was from the Lord and no one else (Psalm 24:8 and Zechariah 10:5).

"True intercessors possessed by the Holy Spirit are as responsible for the victory, as the men and women on the field of battle. Therefore, they had to be dead to the world and all its natural loves and affections; a true crucifixion of the old self, death to self and then resurrection as temples of the Holy Spirit that He and He alone can intercede through for the glory of God. The true burden of intercession with all its sufferings and identification can only be born by the Holy Spirit in spiritual warfare. Flesh will never stand (Romans 8:26-27).

"It is one thing to give your life to Jesus, but all the difference in the world to allow the Person of the Holy Spirit to live His life in you. For He is Holy and will not share His life with the sinful nature of man. When the Holy Spirit engages the enemy in spiritual warfare, the excitement and enthusiasm of the flesh melts into insignificance. There still remains a work on the earth that only the Holy Spirit can bear through the Body of the Church. The gift of the Holy Spirit (the baptism of the Holy Spirit) releases His gifts for works of service to empower as witnesses, first in Jerusalem and then to the ends of the earth, to plant and build up the Church. At the same time, the Holy Spirit is seeking out those who are willing to be cleansed before He can enter them in all His power and fullness, as He lived in Jesus (Luke 4:1-14).

"The Holy Spirit seeks to lead the Church into battle on the earth and in the Heavens above. Moses was led by the Spirit against the Amalekites at Rephidim (Exodus 17). While Joshua led the army of the Lord into battle on the earth claiming the ground beneath their feet, Moses aided by Aaron and Hur interceded on their behalf, led by the Spirit, in conjunction with the angelic forces above the earth, to overcome the principalities and powers of darkness. This was the Church in the wilderness as one body, God's military forces on the earth working in harmony in one accord, one in spirit and mind, one in spirit and in truth. All interdependent, directed by the Spirit of God, who facilitated and coordinated the two armies to bring about victory. The highest Heavens belong to the Lord, but the earth He has given to man (Psalm 115:16). Though you live in the world, you cannot wage war as the world does. The weapons at your disposal have Divine power to bind the strong man and demolish his strongholds, but must be used as directed by the Holy Spirit.

"For most in this generation, prayer has become devalued, debased, demeaned and dishonoured. For most, it has become perverted to nothing more than a wish list of selfish desires of the flesh. Even for many in so called fulltime ministry, intercession is an enigma. Former generations fasted and prayed on their knees humbling themselves, crying out, pleading for the lost, broken-hearted and in tears. There was a deep desire in their hearts to live a holy life. Whereas today, there is almost a siege like mentality, with the Army of the Lord hiding behind four walls and a sinful lifestyle; asking God to send others to join them, to help make up their numbers so that they can keep the lights on, yet sadly have little or no concern for those who live in darkness without the light of the world!

"Spiritual warfare is not for the fainthearted or the few. There are those who believe if they leave the devil alone or deny his existence and don't get involved, somehow he will overlook them and leave them alone. You fools! You are deceived, a sitting target. Did not Jesus' disciples hide behind locked doors for fear of persecution? Yet when the Holy Spirit came upon them with fire, they went out and turned their world upside down. If you cannot stand now and face a faceless foe, how on earth will you face the antichrist – the man of lawlessness, who is coming? The baptism of the Holy Spirit is not a sign of approval but part of an on-going process to create a temple for the Holy Spirit to abide in and when He comes, He comes to live His life without the contention of another, no strife, no debate. He comes to abide and live His life in you exactly as Jesus lived His life while on the earth. This is God's good, pleasing and perfect will for the Body of Christ to be transformed by the Holy Spirit and be conformed into the image of Jesus, and walk in the light, as He is in the light so that the Kingdom of God can come on earth as in Heaven.

"In keeping with the gained place of intercession by the Holy Spirit through Rees and Samuel Rees Howells, and the team of intercessors at the former Bible College of Wales, UK, thousands of intercessors possessed by the Holy Spirit are being raised up in the nations of the world in keeping with God's promise to pour out His Spirit on all flesh. To bind the strong man and pull down his strongholds, to release apostles, prophets, evangelists and all manner of men and women possessed by the Holy Spirit to complete the Every Creature Commission (the Great Commission), to take the gospel to every nation, tribe and tongue in the power of the Holy Spirit. Because of their position in Christ and the gained place of intercession for the finances required, God will provide for all their needs in Christ Jesus for His glory. There is no excuse that is acceptable, every true born again believer should be a disciple and should be involved one way or another."

Michael Backholer, 29 March 2013, (Good Friday, Easter) – www.ProphecyNow.co.uk

This book is also available as an ebook.

www.ByFaith.co.uk

www.ProphecyNow.co.uk

Index to Key Words and Phrases

This index to key words has been produced to include words and phrases that are relevant and most helpful for searching within this book. Within this listing, terms have been added which may not be within this book, but are an allusion to. As examples, the word 'maturity' is not within any prophecy or revelation, but the words 'milk' and 'solid foods' are – the biblical allusion to maturity in Christ. The words 'golf' or 'football' (soccer) are not mentioned but Ryder Cup and the Premier League are. Woods, Tiger has been listed in the index, however within the prophecy it is a play on words, as are many other examples.

In addition, whilst the index is alphabetical in its listings (except People of the Bible which is Chronological), there has been minor deviations to keep related words or phrases together, as in Every Creature and Great Commission to aid search-ability. There are also some veiled references such as the Lakeland Revival and Islam that have also been included. These exact words may not be found on the pages listed, but the allusion to is. On a final note, many of the revivals listed are only referred to within a prophecy by the surname of the person who was at the forefront of the move of the Holy Spirit. Within this index, first names and the full title and year(s) of the revivals have been included in the index only. As an example, Campbell is mentioned, who is Duncan Campbell, the revivalist of the Hebridean Revival (1949-1952).

Intercession (*see also* Warfare), 43, 45, 47, 49, 50, 51, 52, 84, 97, 98, 118, 123, 124, 125.
Every Creature / Every Creature Commission, 45, 46, 48, 49, 52, 54, 83, 94, 95, 99, 122, 125.
Great Commission, 23, 51, 52, 77, 94, 119.
Go and Make Disciples, 36, 83, 118.
Good News, 12, 16, 20, 30, 40, 56, 65, 77, 89, 90, 108, 112, 120, 121.
Gospel, 8, 17, 20, 23, 30, 31, 35, 43, 44, 46, 47, 52, 56, 65, 69, 75, 81, 83, 90, 94, 107, 108, 118, 119.
Maturity (Milk and Solid Food), 80, 89, 120.
Net, 54, 120.
Net (of deception), 53, 120.
Warfare (*see also* Intercession), 32, 43, 44, 45, 46, 47, 50, 94, 95, 118, 122, 123.

Events: (*See also* Revival)
Arab Spring, 107.
Baptism of the Holy Spirit, 77, 98, 102, 114, 123, 124.
Birth Pains, 89, 116.
Carnival / Circus, 84, 86, 92.
Decade of Evangelism, 120.
Football (Soccer) / Premier League, 26.
Fundraising (*see also* Money), 91, 93.
Golf (Ryder Cup), 39.
Spring-Clean, 80, 106, 107.
Second Coming, 12.
Wedding, 25, 87, 88.

People: (*See also* Revivalists)
Bentley, Todd, 63, 65.
Howells, Rees, 44, 45, 46, 47, 50, 52, 84, 99, 122, 123, 125.
Howells, Samuel Rees, 50, 51, 52, 84, 99, 125.
Müller, George, 30.
Netanhyahu, Benjamin, 77.
Obama, Barak, 77.
Wood, Tiger, 39.

People – Others:
Bankers / Politicians / Leaders, 43, 44, 56, 66, 73.
Hidden Ones, 84, 98, 99.
Leaders / Leadership (Those in Spiritual Authority), 43, 56, 66, 73, 99, 109.
Older / Grey Haired, 57.
Shepherd(s) / Pastor(s), 10, 36, 91, 104, 105.
Spiritual Fathers, 30, 31.
Young Ones / Youth, 56, 57, 110, 111.

81, 83, 84, 86, 88, 92, 95, 96, 97, 98, 99, 101, 102, 103, 104, 107, 109, 112, 114, 115, 116, 117, 118, 119, 120, 122, 123, 124, 125.
Lakeland Revival (2008) under Bentley, 63, 64, 65, 120.
Outpourings, 13, 38, 39, 52, 95, 101.
Pentecost, 13, 19, 22, 78, 98, 112.
Pyongyang Great Revival (1907-1910) in Korea, 112, 113.
Revival, chapters 1-2. 23, 32, 32, 39, 54, 63, 66, 74, 91, 98, 104, 112, 113, 120.
Seed Harvest, 16.
Welsh Revival (1904-1905) under Roberts, 19, 39.

Revivalists: (*See also* People)
Bentley, Todd, 63, 64, 65, 120.
Campbell, Duncan, 39.
Edwards, Jonathan, 19, 39.
Finney, Charles, 19, 39, 49.
Wesley, John and Charles, 19, 39.

Significant Dates or Seasons:
07-07-07 (7 July 07), 20, 21.
Christmas (Baubles / Trimming), 87, 88.
Easter, 49, 91, 125.
Father's Day (UK), 101.
Pentecost Sunday, 13, 112.

Other Seasons:
Healing, 12, 47, 54, 73, 100, 101.
Other Seasons, (Combine, Faith, Glory, Outpouring etc.), 37, 41, 42, 44, 46, 57, 58, 72, 98, 101, 110.
Wind of Change, 14, 17, 63, 116.

Technology:
Social Media / Internet / Facebook / Twitter / Digital Technology / Network, 53, 111, 121. (*See also* Media / Television / TV, under Other).

Money:
Economic / Finances / Money, 46, 58, 73, 79, 84, 89, 90, 92, 93, 97, 103, 108, 113, 121, 125.
Fundraising / Pockets with Holes / Silver / Prosperity / Tithes, 53, 58, 81, 82, 91, 92, 93, 97, 113, 116, 118.

Warnings: (*See also* Events)
Church / Bride / Body of Christ (Baubles, Trimmings), chapter 4. 6, 17, 18, 19, 22, 30, 31, 32, 33, 34, 35, 40, 41, 42, 43, 44, 46, 48, 54, 55, 58, 59, 60, 64, 66, 73, 75, 77, 79, 80, 81, 84, 89, 92, 94, 96, 98, 100, 101, 105, 106, 107, 109, 110, 111, 113, 114, 115, 116, 118, 119, 120, 121, 122, 123, 124.

Church / Flock, 84, 91, 104, 105, 106, 116, 109, 124.
Deceiving Spirits / Evil Spirit / Unclean Spirits, 9, 43, 68, 88, 97, 108, 118, 119.
Deception, chapter 20. 39, 73, 75, 88, 92, 94, 96, 97, 102, 107, 111, 112, 114, 115, 119, 120.
Demon(s) / demonic, 21, 26, 43, 56, 77, 93, 97.
False Teachers / Teaching / Prophets, etc., (*see also* Tares and Wolves), 9, 10, 31, 43, 64, 70, 75, 81, 82, 91, 92, 109, 110, 116, 119.
End-Time(s), chapter 12. 12, 13, 22, 43, 44, 46, 52, 56, 57, 58, 71, 72, 73, 74, 77, 95, 101, 104, 115, 116, 123.
Heaven / Heavenly, 10, 12, 13, 19, 20, 21, 22, 24, 25, 27, 28, 32, 36, 37, 40, 44, 46, 49, 51, 53, 54, 56, 57, 58, 63, 70, 71, 73, 75, 97, 106, 112, 115, 116, 117, 118, 120, 122, 123.
Hell, 23, 111, 118, 120.
Judgment, 18, 35, 61, 66, 69, 70, 78.
Sword, 18, 28, 32, 33, 60, 94, 101, 111, 114, 119, 120.
Tare(s), (*see also* False Teachers / Teaching etc. and Wolves), chapter 18. 31, 81, 85, 94, 96, 104, 106, 107, 109, 110, 111, 114, 119, 120.
Wolves, 43, 81, 92, 104, 109, 110, 111.
Weather (Sun, Climate, Tsunami, Global Warming), 13, 16, 23, 45, 48, 61, 72, 86, 88, 96, 100, 101, 109, 113.

Other:
Abortion, 29.
Angel(s), 33, 43, 53, 58, 84, 99, 109, 118, 120, 122, 123.
Bible, 6, 7, 8, 10, 19, 43, 77, 88, 91, 105, 118, 119.
Fruit (Good or Bad / Bacteria) / Fruitful, 16, 19, 31, 33, 47, 50, 52, 55, 58, 74, 75, 80, 81, 86, 93, 94, 100, 102, 104, 105, 113, 115, 117.
Full Surrender / Living Sacrifices, 25, 47, 50, 67, 94, 99, 102, 122.
Garden / Gardening / Nature / Horticulture, 75, 85, 86, 94, 96, 101, 102, 105, 106, 110, 111, 113, 119.
Holiness, 21, 42, 55, 60, 71, 118, 120.
Honey, 101, 119.
Islam, (Cruel Barbaric / Veils), 20, 38-39, 106-107.
Media / Television / TV, 7, 34, 91, 92, 93, 107, 120, 121. (*See also* Social Media, under Technology).
Ministry / Ministries, 8, 10, 30, 53, 59, 76, 77, 82, 84, 93, 110, 114, 117, 124.
Worship (Spirit and in Truth and One in Spirit and in Truth), 28, 40, 51, 52, 53, 54, 94, 86, 95, 114, 123, 124.

www.ByFAITH.co.uk

www.PROPHECYNOW.co.uk

ByFaith Media Books

Revival Fires and Awakenings – Thirty-Six Visitations of the Holy Spirit: A Call to Holiness, Prayer and Intercession for the Nations by Mathew Backholer. With 36 fascinating accounts of revivals in nineteen countries from six continents, plus biblical teaching on revival & prayer etc. Also available as a hardback.

Britain A Christian Country, A Nation Defined by Christianity and the Bible & the Social Changes that Challenge this Biblical Heritage by Paul Backholer.

Heaven – A Journey to Paradise and the Heavenly City by Paul Backholer. What will heaven be like? Experience it now!

Holy Spirit Power – Knowing the Voice, Guidance and Person of the Holy Spirit by Paul Backholer. Power for Christian living.

The Holy Spirit in a Man: Spiritual Warfare, Intercession, Faith, Healings and Miracles by R. B. Watchman.

Tares and Weeds in Your Church: Trouble & Deception in God's House, the End Time Overcomers by R. B. Watchman.

Global Revival, Worldwide Outpourings, Forty-Three Visitations of the Holy Spirit by Mathew Backholer. The author reveals the links between pioneering missionaries and the revivals that they saw in their fulfilment of the Great Commission. With 43 accounts of revival and biblical teaching.

Revival Fire, 150 Years of Revivals: Spiritual Awakenings and Moves of the Holy Spirit by Mathew Backholer. This book documents in detail, twelve revivals from ten countries.

Understanding Revival and Addressing the Issues it Provokes by Mathew Backholer, guides us through centuries of God's Divine visitations and reveals what we can expect to see, as God rends the heavens and pours out His Spirit.

*Revival Answers, True and False Revivals, Genuine or Counterfeit: Do not be Deceived...*by Mathew Backholer.

Celtic Christianity & the First Christian Kings in Britain by Paul Backholer. From St Patrick and King Ethelbert.

Extreme Faith – On Fire Christianity by Mathew Backholer. Discover the powerful biblical foundations for on fire faith. Biblical truths and routines to shake your world!

Jesus Today, Daily Devotional: 100 Days with Jesus Christ by Paul Backholer. Daily Christian Bible inspiration.

How Christianity Made the Modern World by Paul Backholer. Read how Christianity helped create the path that led to Western liberty and laid the foundations of the modern world.

Samuel Rees Howells: A Life of Intercession by Richard Maton is an in-depth look at the intercessions of Samuel Howells and the faith principles that he learnt from his father, Rees Howells and from the Holy Spirit. With 39 photos in the paperback and hardback editions.

Samuel, Son and Successor of Rees Howells: Director of the Bible College of Wales – A Biography by Richard Maton. The author invites us on a lifelong journey with Samuel, to unveil his ministry at the College, his life of prayer and College friends, as the history of BCW unfolds alongside the Vision to reach Every Creature with the Gospel. With 113 black and white photos in the paperback and hardback editions.

Short-Term Mission, A Christian Guide to STMs: For Leaders, Pastors, Churches, Students, STM Teams and Mission Organizations by Mathew Backholer.

How to Plan, Prepare and Successfully Complete your Short-Term Mission by Mathew Backholer. From his many adventures in over 35 nations, Mathew reveals how to plan well, avoid the pitfalls and successfully complete your STM!

The Exodus Evidence In Pictures – The Bible's Exodus: The Hunt for Ancient Israel in Egypt, the Red Sea, the Exodus Route and Mount Sinai by Paul Backholer. With 100 colour photos in the paperback edition.

The Ark of the Covenant – Investigating the Ten Leading Claims by Paul Backholer. Join two explorers as they investigate the location of antiquities greatest relic. With 80+ exclusive colour photos in the paperback edition.

ByFaith Media DVDs

Great Christian Revivals on DVD is an inspirational and uplifting account of some of the greatest revivals in Church history. Filmed in England, Scotland and Wales and drawing upon archive information, including historic photos, computer animation and depictions, the stories of the Welsh Revival (1904-1905), the Hebridean Revival (1949-1952) and the Evangelical Revival (1739-1791) are brought to life in this moving 72-minutes documentary.

ByFaith – World Mission DVD is an 85-minute compelling reality TV documentary that reveals the real experiences of a backpacking style Christian short-term mission in Asia, Europe and North Africa. Filmed over three years, *ByFaith – World Mission* is the very best of ByFaith TV – season one.

Israel in Egypt – The Exodus Mystery on 1 DVD. A four year quest searching for Joseph, Moses and the Hebrew slaves in Egypt. Join Paul and Mathew as they hunt through ancient relics and explore the mystery of the biblical exodus, hunt for the Red Sea and climb Mt. Sinai. Discover the first reference to Israel outside of the Bible, uncover depictions of people with multicolour coats, encounter the Egyptian records of slaves making bricks and find lost cities. 110 minutes. The best of *ByFaith – In Search of the Exodus*.

ByFaith – Quest for the Ark of the Covenant on 1 DVD. Join two adventurers on their quest for the Ark, beginning at Mount Sinai where it was made, to Pharaoh Tutankhamun's tomb, where Egyptian treasures evoke the majesty of the Ark. The quest proceeds onto the trail of Pharaoh Shishak, who raided Jerusalem. The mission continues up the River Nile to find a lost temple, with clues to a mysterious civilisation. Crossing through the Sahara Desert, the investigators enter the underground rock churches of Ethiopia, find a forgotten civilisation and examine the enigma of the final resting place of the Ark itself. 100+ minutes.

www.ByFaithDVDs.co.uk

www.ByFaith.co.uk

Notes

Lightning Source UK Ltd.
Milton Keynes UK
UKOW06f2347270616

277220UK00016B/487/P